CACTI AND SUCCULENTS

The American Horticultural Society
Illustrated Encyclopedia of Gardening

CACTI AND SUCCULENTS

The American Horticultural Society
Mount Vernon, Virginia

For The American Horticultural Society

President
Dr. Gilbert S. Daniels

Technical Advisory Committee
Everett Conklin
Mary Stuart Maury
Dr. John A. Wott

Cacti and Succulents Staff for The Franklin Library/Ortho Books

Editorial Director
Min S. Yee

Supervisory Editor
Lewis P. Lewis

Editor
Ken Burke

Associate Editor
Bonnie Cutler

Art Directors
John Williams
Barbara Ziller

Creative Director
Michael Mendelsohn

Assistant Creative Director
Clint Anglin

Written by
Alice Quiros
Barbara L. Young

Contributing Writer
Martha Baker

Special Consultants
Robert Causey
Robert Foster
Edward and Betty Gay
Sara Godwin
Murray Goldmintz
Burt Greenberg
Margaret Brandstrom Pavel
Harold and Miriam Ritzfield

Illustrations by
Leavitt Dudley
Ron Hildebrand

Production Director
Robert Laffler

Production Manager
Renee Guilmette

Production Assistant
Paula Green

For Ortho Books

Publisher
Robert L. Iacopi

For The Franklin Library

Publisher
Joseph Sloves

The cactus shown on the cover is a particularly beautiful example of the *Lobovia* hybrid 'Red Riding Hood'. Photograph copyright © 1982 by Derek Fell.

Major Photography by
William Aplin
Michael Landis

Additional Photography by
Abbey Garden Press
Martha Baker
Dr. G. Barad
Ernest Braun
Clyde Childress
Fred Lyon
Michael McKinley

Crafts Design, page 79
Florence Sullivan

Acknowledgments

Eleanor Barker
Palos Verdes, California

Priscilla Beattie
Pasadena, California

John and Mary Bleck
Abbey Gardens
Carpenteria, California

Betty Chapman
Redondo Beach, California

Dr. Bernard Deutsch
New York, New York

Fuschia Land Nursery
Los Angeles, California

Charlotte Gallay
Los Angeles, California

Charles Glass
Santa Barbara, California

Harriet and Murray Goldmintz
New York, New York

Burt Greenberg
Cycadia
Northridge, California

Ben Haines
Topeka, Kansas

Indian Rock Nursery
Vista, California

Myron Kimnach
Huntington Botanic Gardens
San Marino, California

La Cienega Nursery
Los Angeles, California

Lila Lillie
Lila's Succulents
San Rafael, California

Louise Lippold
Locust Valley, New York

Bruce Miller
Northridge, California

Stan Oleson
San Pedro, California

Victoria Padilla
Los Angeles, California

Red Desert
San Francisco, California

Harold and Miriam Ritzfield
Englewood, New Jersey

Joe and Patti Rubio
San Pedro, California

George Schmidt
Torrance, California

Silhouettes of the Desert
Vista, California

M. R. Stern

Dr. and Mrs. True

Rogers Weld
Fernwood Plants
Topanga, California

Henk Worries
Palos Verdes, California

George and Annie Yasui
Honolulu, Hawaii

Produced under the authorization of The American Horticultural Society by The Franklin Library and Ortho Books.

Copyright © 1974, 1977, by Ortho Books. Special contents © 1982 by The American Horticultural Society. All rights reserved under International and Pan-American Copyright Conventions.

Every effort has been made at the time of publication to guarantee the accuracy of the names and addresses of information sources and suppliers and in the technical data contained. However, the subscriber should check for his own assurance and must be responsible for selection and use of suppliers and supplies, plant materials, and chemical products.

No portion of this book may be reproduced in any form or by any means without permission first being requested and obtained in writing from The American Horticultural Society, c/o The Franklin Library, Franklin Center, Pennsylvania, 19091. Portions of this volume previously appeared in the Ortho Books *House Plants Indoors/Outdoors* and *The World of Cactus & Succulents*.

Library of Congress Catalog Card Number 82−71929

Printed in the United States of America

12 11 10 9 8 7 6 5

A Special Message from
The American Horticultural Society

Cacti and Succulents introduces you to the wonders of the botanical world—those plants that require a minimum amount of water, flourish almost anywhere, and please the eye with their dramatic forms. Developing a lush, healthy succulent collection is easy, regardless of the time and area you have to devote to it, and this volume provides you with the techniques to do so.

Starting with the basics, you'll learn about potting soils, when to water and feed, and how to choose the right containers for your succulents. You'll also find information on diseases and pests, plus practical prevention know-how. Of course, the amount of light a plant gets is extremely important; find out about natural and artificial light and how it affects the color, size, and growing habits of succulents. To help you increase your collection, methods of propagation and culture are also included.

Your imagination will be stimulated when you discover the wide array of succulents. From the majestic giant saguaro cactus to the beautifully flowering kalanchoe, there is a succulent to suit any gardener's taste. The detailed descriptions and photographs in this book will help you create a unique, elegant environment inside and outside your home. Read about growing succulents with the bonsai look, for instance, or learn how to make unusual plant containers to accent a table or a patio. Whether you live in an apartment or have a generous amount of space, whether you are a novice or an experienced gardener, you will come across many ideas that will beautify your surroundings. Even if you live in a cold climate, you can landscape with winter-hardy succulents or enjoy a lovely greenhouse.

The "Encyclopedia of Succulents" will be invaluable when you make your plant selection. Each listing shows the plant, and gives its botanical name, family, group, and origin, plus general and flower descriptions, information on propagation and culture, and recommended species. You can also find out where to purchase the plants of your choice by referring to the section on mail-order succulent nurseries.

With the information in *Cacti and Succulents*, you will be well on your way to experiencing the joy of growing these remarkable plants. You'll soon learn that a little time and effort yields tremendous results.

Gilbert S. Daniels
President

CONTENTS

This chapter introduces you to water-thrifty plants and gives some reasons for their development. Here also are general rules regarding watering requirements and an explanation of the difference between cacti and succulents. Discover the wide variety of succulent plants—you will see that there is something for any gardener in any environment.

The growth of a healthy succulent depends on choosing a sturdy specimen at a reputable nursery, potting it in the proper soil mix and container, and giving it the right amount of water and light. Learn how to determine what your particular growing conditions are, plus methods of fertilizing and feeding, controlling pests and disease, and propagating new plants.

Succulents, Indoors and Out

Plant a lush succulent landscape as an alternative to a lawn, decorate your home with succulent "sculpture," or design a greenhouse for a year-round garden. These versatile plants can thrive almost anywhere with relatively little care, under natural or artificial light, potted or not. See which ones are recommended for specific situations.

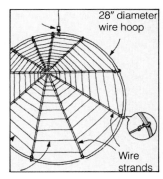  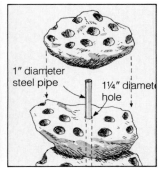

Developing a Collection

Here you will find advice on how to create unique displays for your succulents, from selecting the perfect container for a single plant, to building a vertical volcanic garden. There are even tips on what to do with trimmings. As collecting becomes an increasingly important part of your life, space can become a problem. Find out from experts how to accommodate the overflow.

Encyclopedia of Succulents

Select the plants that appeal to you. You will find photographs, detailed descriptions, and information on cultural needs for scores of succulents.

SUCCULENTS–THE IDEAL PLANTS

The special characteristics of succulents make a special kind of gardening possible, full of wonderful colors, fascinating textures, and extraordinary shapes.

Every gardener dreams of the ideal plant—one that has interesting structure and beautiful flowers, thrives on neglect, draws gasps of admiration from the neighbors, and comes in enough varieties to fascinate for a lifetime. The ideal plant is, in short, a succulent.

Succulents are like self-made people—successful in spite of adversity, overcoming the odds. These stubborn individualists of the plant world have adapted to great climatic changes over millions of years. The methods of survival that have evolved are unique to succulents and curious by any standard.

All succulents store water in their leaves, stems, or both. This is what makes them succulents and is itself an evolutionary development. But the way in which they store or obtain the water varies, the variations being dictated by the climatic conditions of their native habitat. Some succulents developed disproportionately thick rootstocks to store moisture and nourishment for periods of drought and searing sun. Where a previously dry or moderately dry habitat gradually became wetter, many succulents evolved into tree-living plants called epiphytes; they began to use their roots for gripping trees to adapt to a dryer microclimate rather than drawing nourishment from the damp and inhospitable ground. Their leaves absorbed moisture from the air. Still other succulents adapted to rocky or frigid environments.

Not all succulents are arid-area types, such as the desert cacti. Some grow in tropical climates where there are long dry seasons, followed by short but intense rainy seasons, which in turn are followed by periods when the ground becomes increasingly dry but the atmosphere remains humid. These climates produce cacti such as the pencil cactus (*Rhipsalis* species) and the orchid cactus (*Epiphyllum* species). The lily family is also represented by succulents such as the well-known aloes (*Aloe barbadensis*, popular for treating burns), the elephant's foot tree or ponytail (*Beaucarnea recurvata*) from Mexico, and the mother-in-law's tongue (*Sansevieria* species).

If the key to a succulent's success could be summed up in a brief description, it would be "water thrifty." Succulents have mastered the art of water conservation. By reducing their leaf surface to minimize water loss from transpiration (the plant equivalent of breathing and perspiration), and by storing water in their stems or leaves, succulents can control both the amount of water they need and the amount they use.

There are other water-thrifty plants besides succulents. The desert wildflowers that make such a brilliant display immediately following the seasonal rains have adapted to a limited water supply by establishing a pattern of a brief growing season followed by a long dormancy. Succulents can indeed be considered the camels of the plant kingdom.

An example of a different kind of evolutionary survival technique is in the *Lithops* species. These succulents are commonly called "living stones" be-

This flat of succulent seedlings shows the symmetry found in many species.

cause they look amazingly like real ones, a successful form of disguise since those plants that do not look like stones are more readily eaten by animals.

Watering Requirements

Most succulents will tolerate practically anything except foot traffic and overwatering. Since their unusual forms are all adaptations to very little water, they have less than normal moisture requirements.

But this doesn't mean that they don't need water at all. All plants need water. Succulents grown in containers require more frequent watering than those grown in the ground. Depending upon the pots you are using—large or small, clay or plastic, light-colored or dark—the water requirements of your container-grown succulents will vary. In cool or cloudy weather, they don't suffer water stress as quickly as in the hot sunshine. The less sun and heat, the less evaporation there will be from both pot and plant. Careful observation and experience will help you determine your plants' needs.

If you are familiar with any succulents—even if only hen-and-chickens, jade plant, or ice plant come to mind—you probably already know that most of them are structurally dramatic, have interesting growth habits, require little care, and are almost pest-free. The photographs in this book will give you a sampling of the vast and intriguing variety of size, shape, texture, and color that awaits your discovery.

Succulents Versus Cacti

The difference between succulents and cacti is really quite simple: "succulent" is the descriptive term for all plants that store water in their leaves or stems; "cactus" is the name of a large family of plants, nearly all of which are succulent. The rule is: almost all cacti are succulents, but not all succulents are cacti.

The springtime blooms of *Mammillaria* 'Pink Nymph' brighten a flat of the mound-shaped cacti.

Opposite: Brilliant blooms of a succulent dominate a garden corner.

Long, slender *Cephalocereus palmeri* has
both sharp, stiff spines and soft, hairy spines,
which develop as the plant matures.

Contrary to popular belief, spines are not the distinguishing characteristic between cacti and succulents. There are cacti that are not prickly, and prickly succulents that are not cacti. Cacti have areoles (spine cushions), and other succulents—even if they are spiny—lack these spine cushions. Plants are classified into botanical families on the basis of their reproductive systems—not by external characteristics such as leaf form, flower color, habitat, or even degree of prickliness.

The most significant families with succulent members are:

Cactaceae. Almost completely succulent, this family of plants—cacti—rarely has leaves. Those with leaves are the least succulent, which also means that they are less specialized in their adaptation to dry conditions and are thus considered more primitive. Cacti have cushionlike areoles that may be covered with wool, hair, or small bristles, and may be spiny. The flowers usually appear at the areoles, and tend to be large and showy.

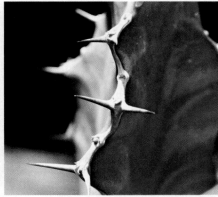

The spine cushion, or areole, distinguishes cacti like *Ritterocereus pruinosis* (far left) from other succulents such as *Euphorbia pseudocactus* (left).

Below: A bed of *Echinocactus grusonii* (golden barrel cactus), illuminated by early morning light, has an otherworldly look.

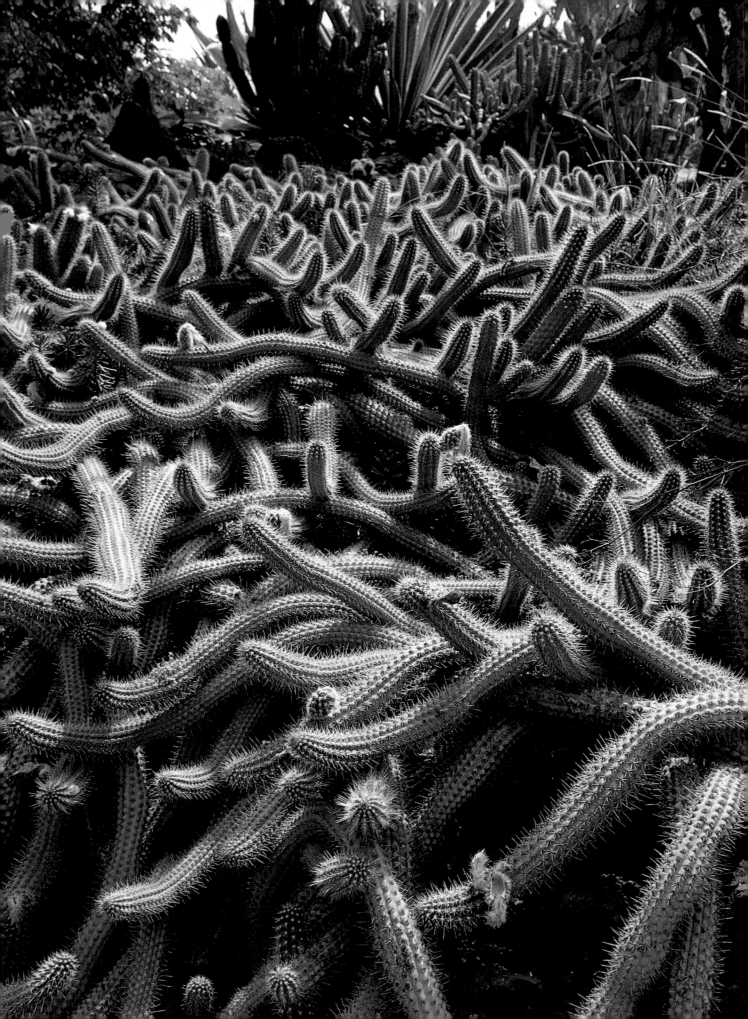

Aizoaceae. Formerly called the Mesembryanthemaceae, this family is exclusively composed of succulents, native to South and Southwest Africa. The flowers look something like daisies, and are large, bright, and colorful.

These plants have adapted to dry growing conditions in a number of ways. Some look shrubby and somewhat woody, with many succulent leaves in opposite pairs at right angles to each other—for example, *Lampranthus* species. At the other extreme are plants that have virtually no stems and only a few pairs of leaves. Examples include *Faucaria, Glottiphylum*, and *Pleiospilos*. Some of these plants ended up with only two leaves, which are partly joined. The more exaggerated version has the leaves forming a solid mass, with only a groove or slit left to mark the boundary line between the leaves. The flowers frequently are larger than the body of the plant. Other plants look like stones in shape and color, and are, in fact, called "living stones" or "stone mimics." Examples include *Conophytum, Lithops*, and *Ophthalmophyllum*.

Crassulaceae. This family contains many species of hardy succulents. The leaves appear in opposite pairs at right angles, or in rosettes, or spirally along the stem. Flowers usually are borne in a cluster. The genus *Sempervivum* is hardy, but the closely related genera *Aeonium* and *Greenovia* are tender. Other genera include *Adromischus, Cotyledon, Crassula, Echeveria, Kalanchoe, Pachyphytum*, and *Sedum*.

Asclepiadaceae. Not all members of this family are succulent, and those that are tend to come from Africa and, to a lesser degree, from India. Many of them, such as *Stapelia*, have no leaves and resemble cacti. The flowers tend to be quite spectacular as are, for example, the flowers of *Ceropegia*, which look like umbrellas.

Compositae. This family has different succulent forms that have adapted to drought to varying degrees. This is one of the largest plant families, with

Left: An *Aeonium* growing in an old stone wall offers a perfect example of symmetry in nature.

Opposite: The procumbent stems of *Trichocereus thelogonus* can stretch as far as 20 or 30 feet.

species in nearly all parts of the world; many of the more interesting succulent forms come from Africa.

Euphorbiaceae. Generally these look like cacti, but their flowers are different, and the stored water is milky. The range of form varies greatly: some plants are woody, some are herbaceous, with ordinary leaves; some have only a few leaves, and succulent, cactuslike stems; others have no leaves at all.

Liliaceae. These plants tend to have a rosette pattern, with a central woody stem surrounded by a whorl of leaves. *Aloe* is one example; other genera include *Gasteria* (the leaves appear in two rows) and *Haworthia* (this has a variety of small rosette plants, including some "window" plants).

Bromeliaceae. All members of this purely American plant family are rosette plants. A few will grow short trunks with age. While most species are succulents, the Bromeliaceae have developed three different methods for storing water. Some of the terrestrial genera, such as *Hechtia* and *Dyckia*, have thick succulent leaves like *Agave* or *Aloe*. Many of the terrestrial and epiphytic species have developed watertight rosettes, which hold water in a tank or reservoir formed by the leaves of the rosette. Finally, a large number of epiphytic species, particularly in the genus *Tillandsia*, have developed specialized scales that cover the leaves. The scales, which give the plants a characteristic soft, gray appearance, can rapidly absorb rainwater, or even fog.

Other families with succulent members include Agavacae, Apocynaceae, Cycadaceae, Discoreaceae, Fouquieriaceae, Geraniaceae, Portulacaceae, and Vitaceae.

Something for Everyone

The apartment gardener who has only a sunny windowsill; the commuter who needs patient, undemanding plants; the collector looking for the unusual; the arts-and-crafts enthusiast who creates with plants—all will find succulents to be absorbing and satisfying. Thousands of succulents offer an amazing variety of color, form, size, and drought resistance. It is entirely possible to become a succulent buff without ever tangling with a prickly one. This rich variety accounts for the wide appeal of succulents.

Do you want a single stunning piece of living sculpture for your office? Try an elkhorn euphorbia (*Euphorbia lactea*). Do you want an exquisite pale green rosette that doesn't require spraying and pruning? Try *Aeonium* species. How about growing Boston beans (*Sedum stahlii*) in the front yard? If you have a flair for the exotic, you may want Hottentot fig (*Carpobrotus*). Maybe you'd like to go in for manufacturing tequila in a small way—plant some blue agave (*Agave tequilana*) and wait patiently (about 25 years).

If you're an armchair traveler, a collection of orchid cacti will inspire many an imaginary jungle expedition. An orchid cactus in bloom, with its fragrant 6-inch-wide flowers, will probably give you a reputation as a horticultural genius. So will a night-blooming cactus—for an unusual treat for you and your friends, stand watch over your *Hylocereus undatus* as it unfolds its cream-white blossoms and perfumes the night air.

If an African safari is beyond your budget, how about a collection of the curiously succulent South African plants? Choose from those with exotic names, such as elephant's foot (*Dioscorea elephantipes*). Perhaps you're a busy city dweller with a small apartment, who has little spare time and even less space. Succulents are remarkably undemanding, and many of them are content to remain in the same pot for years. And as container plants, virtually all of them can exist, if not thrive, in the normally dry, warm atmosphere of the average home.

Succulents come in a vast variety of sizes, from a 60-foot-high saguaro cactus to tiny living stones (lithops), scarcely distinguishable from pebbles. The shapes vary from formal, fluted columns to plump, little baby toes; from

Opposite: *Rhipsalis capilliformus* cascading from a planter belies the vision many people have of cacti as spiny and geometric, but it is a cactus.

Whether in glowing, sometimes nearly iridescent tones (top right) or creamy pastels (far right), cacti can produce spectacular displays of color equal to flowering annuals. Many succulents add bright leaves to a garden display (bottom right).

Opposite: The bright flowers of portulaca (*Portulaca grandiflora*) open in full sun and close at night. Started from seed, this annual succulent can be grown in very dry soil.

The star-shaped bishop's-cap, *Astrophytum myriostigma*.

long-haired cylinders to sculptured rosettes. There are many that you may know already, and many more that you'll enjoy meeting—old-man cactus (*Cephalocereus senilis*), painted-lady (*Echeveria derenbergii*), bishop's-cap (*Astrophytum myriostigma*), and drunkard's dream (*Hatiora salicornioides*).

Whether you want the extraordinary or the ordinary, the strange or the beautiful, there's a collection of succulents for indoors or out that will intrigue you for years.

The encyclopedia on pages 92–138 offers a more comprehensive view of these water-thrifty wonders, but here is a brief sampling of interesting and useful cacti and succulents.

Mistletoe or pencil cactus. These succulents, known as *Rhipsalis*, are strange in appearance, but they are epiphytes growing on the trees, unlike true mistletoe, which is a parasite with its roots growing in the trunk of the tree. They're useful in baskets, pots, and planters. Most are grown for their bright green foliage, but in season the blooms are an added treat, followed by attractive berries, which may last for several months. They thrive in a moist atmosphere with some shade. *Hatiora* (drunkard's dream) is related, and is also fun to grow.

Orchid cacti. These beautiful flowers are as lovely as orchids, but shaped more like water lilies. The stems are flattened and leaflike, not cactuslike, and some make great basket plants in a semishady spot. *Epiphyllum* is the genus, and the most common species, *E. oxypetalum*, is one of the easiest of the so-called night-blooming cereus. Specialists selling locally or by mail order can recommend small-growing hybrids best suited to growing indoors in freezing weather, or larger species that can be grown outdoors in hanging baskets in frost-free areas.

Other cacti. Serious collectors spend years searching out odd and unusual cacti. They've been so successful, in fact, that it may be bewildering to have

to choose only a few plants. The best way is to visit a cactus nursery (or study their catalogs), and select those plants you find most appealing. You may enjoy *Aporocactus, Astrophytum, Chamaecereus, Notocactus, Echinocereus, Opuntia, Echinopsis, Gymnocalycium, Rebutia, Lobivia,* and *Mammillaria*.

Indoors, these all need as much direct sun as you can give them. Outdoors, they can take sun all day, or as little as half a day. To maintain them indoors in a dim area, spotlight them with incandescent floodlights placed about 4 feet away and kept on 14 hours daily.

Agave. This famous succulent belongs to its own family, the Agavaceae. The true century plant, *Agave americana,* is too large for most container gardens except while it is young. Better for long-term pot growing are *A. americana* cultivars 'Marginata' and 'Medio-picta,' *A. desmettiana, A. pumila,* and *A. victoriae-reginae*. These dramatic rosette plants are great accents for patios, terraces, steps, or balconies.

Sedum. Choose from among hundreds of species, all of which do well in containers. Favorites include *S. pachyphyllum* (jelly bean), *S. treleasei, S. × rubrotinctum, S. stahlii, S. dasyphyllum* (miniature creeper), and *S. multiceps* (little Joshua tree). A wonderful basket plant is *S. morganianum*. Shield it from wind and broiling sun; it likes a moister atmosphere.

Stone plants. These incredible little succulents look as if they belong to the mineral kingdom. Collect species of *Conophytum, Dinteranthus, Lithops, Lophophora,* and *Pleiospilos,* then have fun searching for look-alike stones to place in pots with them. They can be grown indoors or outdoors, also in fluorescent-lighted gardens. Some have daisylike flowers.

Wax plant. The leaves and fragrant flowers of *Hoya* are thick and waxy. They make great basket and vine plants. Choicest are variegated forms of *H. carnosa* and miniature *H. bella*.

Windowed succulents. These wonders of nature, related to the stone plants, have translucent "window" areas in the top of each fat, clublike leaf. One popular kind is *Fenestraria aurantiaca,* which grows less than 2 inches tall. Some more common haworthias, such as *Haworthia cymbiformis,* also have translucent leaf tips. In nature the "windows" admit light to sand-covered plants.

Other succulents. Some of these are one-of-a-kind plants; others represent whole families you can have fun exploring. All thrive in container culture, indoors and outdoors; all need frost-free winter quarters. Commonly available are: *Adromischus, Aeonium* (some resemble bronzy red-and-green roses), *Aptenia* (an easy basket plant), *Beaucarnea* (ponytail; an outstanding houseplant), *Cotyledon, Faucaria* (tiger jaws), *Gasteria, Kleinia, Pedilanthus,* and *Senecio rowleyanus* (string-of-beads).

A variety of succulents creates a vivid, highly textured hillside rock garden.

The natural continuance of a species:
undaunted by the spines, a bee pollinates
a *Mammillaria* blossom.

BASIC CARE AND PROPAGATION

You only need to follow a few basic rules to be able to grow succulents easily and successfully. With the information here you can start and enjoy your succulent plants and keep them healthy.

Good cultural practices *don't* begin at home—they start even before you bring your succulents back to your collection. One of the best ways to develop a healthy collection is to buy healthy plants, either from a local nursery or plant shop dealer or a reputable mail-order nursery.

When choosing a plant at the nursery, take a good look at it; you want to bring home the healthiest specimen you can find. Look for the sturdiest plant, not the biggest. Give it a gentle tug to see if it's well rooted. Be sure it has no broken or scarred leaves. Check for insect pests, such as mealybugs or scale. When you get your plant home, knock it out of the pot and take a look at the soil.

Succulents are often potted in lightweight soil mixes for shipping and handling. These are adequate to maintain the plant during the distribution process from grower to retailer to you; however, plants might need to be repotted with another rooting medium before they become a permanent part of your collection. Because succulents are frequently top-heavy, sometimes plaster of Paris has been used to stabilize the plant to prevent it from being damaged if knocked over. If you find your plant firmly embedded in a hard, white lump, don't worry—it's only plaster of Paris. It's water soluble, so just take the plant out of the pot and soak the rootball until the plaster of Paris comes apart. Once the root system can be worked free, repot the plant in the soil mix appropriate to the species. (See charts, pages 32 and 33).

If you buy from specialty nurseries that stock *only* succulents, their plants will probably be properly potted in an appropriate soil mix and pot. Mail-order specialty nurseries are a good source for hard-to-find varieties. Plants are often sent bareroot, along with instructions for potting and maintenance. Pot these as soon as you receive them. Keep newly potted plants on the dry side for the first few weeks to prevent any rot from starting on damaged root surfaces. The best way to find a reliable mail-order source is to check with other collectors in your area for recommendations. If you aren't familiar with the source, place only a small test order. If the plants and service are satisfactory, you will probably find them just as good on a more extensive order. Shipped plants are usually small, and for good reason—younger plants are easier to re-establish in a new environment. They develop new roots sooner and grow faster than mature plants of the same species. A fully mature, ready-to-bloom plant takes much longer to readjust and, under less than expert care, might not survive the transition.

Soil Mixes

Most successful collectors keep two or three containers of prepared soil mixes, or the ingredients for soil mixes, readily available for short-notice potting jobs. Kept in covered containers and protected from soil pests and excess moisture, the prepared soils, or their ingredients, are ready and waiting when new arrivals turn up. A trowel and a stockpile of clean,

Spines and hair help reduce evaporation and provide shade.

sterilized pots in a variety of sizes complete the list of useful items to have on hand for potting.

To keep succulents healthy, a soil mix must have three essentials: moisture retention, drainage (aeration), and nourishment. The soil must retain sufficient moisture to dissolve nutrients so they can be absorbed by the roots.

Drainage is the soil's ability to drain off excess moisture immediately in order to provide for adequate aeration. Roots need a balance of water and air in the soil to survive. If given too much water, the roots "drown" and rot; if given too little, the roots starve and the plant dehydrates. Either extreme will kill the plant. If, however, you are inclined toward extremes, it's better to sin in the direction of too little water than too much. The formulas given for soil mixes in this chapter will assure you of a fast-draining, well-aerated soil.

The third element, nourishment, is the variable. Although all succulents must have adequate moisture and excellent aeration, they vary in the amount of nourishment they require. As a rule, the jungle species (tropical epiphytes), such as *Rhipsalis* or *Epiphyllum*, require a richer soil than do the desert, alpine, or shoreline species. A few—and these are a small minority of succulents—thrive best in a very lean or low-nutrient growing medium. The cultural charts on pages 32 and 33 indicate which soil mix is appropriate to each species.

You could talk to ten experienced growers and come up with ten different soil-mix formulas for succulents. To forestall this, three basic ingredients are described here, as well as the purposes they serve. Acceptable substitutes are also suggested, some of which may be available in your area. Some you may never have heard of before, but all have their advocates. You can take your choice in terms of cost and availability.

Potting Soil as a Basic

Plants from the desert need a gritty, lean, growing medium. Most cacti and other succulents will prosper in a mixture of 1 part soil, 1 part sand (not beach sand but coarse "builder's sand"), ½ part decayed leaf mold, and ½ part crushed clay flowerpot or brick. To each half bushel of mixture, add a cup each of ground horticultural limestone and bone meal.

The base for almost any potting mix is soil. Use any packaged sterilized potting soil or artificial soil mix. There are several brands, all equally good. You can find them at garden centers and nurseries. They have the advantages of coming in convenient sizes and being disease, pest, and weed-free. Consider a packaged soil as your basic ingredient, but not as a complete soil. When used by itself, it retains too much moisture for succulents. You can substitute good garden loam if you have it, or your local nursery may offer its own sterilized soil or artificial soil mix, which will do as well.

Drainage. Coarse sand is an ingredient used to provide aeration and drainage. It is often available at builder's supply centers. Be sure to get a coarse grade; fine sand packs down hard, eliminating air spaces. It also crusts over on the surface, making it hard for water to penetrate. Again, don't use beach sand—it's much too fine and salty.

Many growers use sponge rock to provide drainage and aeration because it is lightweight and does not compact. It keeps the soil porous and fast-draining. Succulents tend to be slow-growing plants and do not need to be repotted frequently unless the soil compacts and drainage becomes poor.

Sponge rock does have one inconvenient feature: it is so lightweight that it floats off the surface of the soil when you water. Therefore, some growers prefer a fine grade of crushed volcanic rock, which is slightly heavier. Like sponge rock, it does not break down in the soil and will provide fast drainage over a period of years. It is available at garden centers in either black or red. Except for the color, there is no difference between the two.

Other substitutes for coarse sand are perlite, silt-free decomposed granite, and coarsely crushed charcoal. Pet stores carry activated charcoal in small amounts, and farm-supply stores stock poultry charcoal. Agricultural pumice (mined from an area in the California desert) is preferred by many commercial succulent growers to coarse sand or perlite. Because it does not break down, it permanently prohibits soil from shrinking or compacting. It is stable in the pot, so it doesn't float like perlite or wash down like sand.

Nutrients. The last essential ingredient is leaf mold (compost). This gives the potting mix bulk and texture and releases nutrients to the plant over a considerable period of time. If you have a yard, a compost heap will provide a free supply from your garden leftovers—leaves, grass clippings, any vegetable kitchen waste. If leaf mold isn't available, you can substitute some sphagnum moss; you'll find it at nurseries and garden centers. Note that sphagnum moss and peat moss are not the same, and peat moss will not do. It's too acidic, it compacts, and it retains moisture too long.

Using these ingredients, you can make up a potting soil that will suit any succulent—just vary the proportions of each ingredient. The three soil mixes recommended here will take care of the needs of a wide variety of species. Check the cultural charts on pages 32 and 33 for the mixture appropriate to the plant you're potting up.

Basic recipes

#1 Extra lean—A low-nutrient formula

  2 parts coarse sand or
    agricultural pumice
  1 part potting soil

#2 Regular—A general formula

  1 part coarse sand or agricultural
    pumice
  1 part potting soil
  1 part leaf mold

#3 Extra rich—A high-nutrient formula

  1 part coarse sand or agricultural
    pumice
  1 part potting soil
  2 parts leaf mold

Containers. New plastic or glazed pots can be used immediately, but soak new clay pots before using them. This will keep the pot from absorbing water from the soil.

If you'll be planting in used pots, scrub and sterilize them first. Scrubbing is considerably easier if you soak the pot before you start to scrub. Sterilizing can be done quickly by using the drying cycle of the dishwasher.

If you use bleach or some chemical to sterilize your pots, be sure to rinse them thoroughly before using them. One cactus expert who uses only clay pots soaks them in rainwater for 24 hours after sterilizing them chemically. Nonporous pots, such as plastic or glazed containers, do not need soaking after sterilizing because they do not absorb the chemicals that can burn the roots.

What size should you use? This is determined by the shape and size of the plant. Tall, shrubby, or cylindrical plants should have pots half as wide as the height of the plant, so that an 8-inch plant should have a pot 4 inches in diameter. Globular plants should have a pot 1 inch wider around than the plant, so that a golden barrel cactus 12 inches across needs a 13-inch pot. (The size of a pot is determined by its top diameter.)

It's not always possible to find a pot that's precisely the right size, but you

A large strawberry pot is easily transformed into a container for succulents.

should try to come as close as possible. The plant needs room for root growth and space for watering at the top. You can compensate for an oversized pot by adding more drainage material in the soil mixture. This ensures that the soil will not remain too wet too long.

To give your plants a long and healthy life, keep these factors in mind when choosing a container:

☐ The size of the pot should be compatible with the size and shape of the plant.
☐ Porous pots (clay) dry out more quickly than nonporous pots.
☐ The drainage hole should be adequate to allow fast drainage.

The potting process. Potting is much easier when your materials are organized and you follow the routine outlined below.

1. Check your new plant for pests to be sure it's clean and healthy before introducing it to the rest of your collection.
2. Prepare your soil mixture before unpotting your new plant.
3. Choose a scrubbed, sterilized container. Cut a piece of wire mesh—old window screening is perfect—large enough to cover the drainage hole with an overlap of ¼ inch all around. The purpose of the mesh is to allow water to drain out without washing away the soil. Place a curved piece of broken clay pot over the screened drainage hole as an added precaution against soil washing out or clogging the screen and slowing down drainage.
4. Moisten some potting mix slightly and make a small pad or layer of soil in the bottom of the pot. The soil should be crumbly damp, not soaked. Wet soil is an open invitation to root rot.

To plant a succulent like this *Echeveria* species (top left), select a container based on root size and scale of plant (top right). Soak clay pots before planting. Place a layer of broken pottery, small gravel, or charcoal chips in the bottom of the container (middle left). Add sterile soil to pot, loosen soil around plant roots, and set plant in position (middle right). Add soil to fill pot, packing firmly to eliminate air pockets, leaving room for watering (bottom left). Clean plant and pot and add a mulch (sand or gravel) if desired (bottom right). Succulents should not be watered for a few days after transplanting.

Spines can pierce garden gloves, so wrap a prickly cactus with thick rolled newspaper for easy handling (far left). Use a spoon to add soil in tight places (center) and a fork to pack soil (left). Clean soil from the plant with a small paintbrush. Don't water cacti for a few days after transplanting.

5. Knock the plant out of the pot. Check the rootball for pests or damaged roots. Cut away any broken, dead, or diseased roots with a pair of sterilized pruning scissors like the ones florists use for cutting stems. Rub the shoulders of the rootball gently to remove the hard crust at the base of the stem. Squeeze the rootball gently to crumble away any soil not adhering to the roots.
6. Pick up the plant, supporting the stem so it doesn't break under its own weight.
7. Center the plant in the pot, making sure the soil does not cover the stem or trunk. Always maintain the same soil level at which the plant was growing before. Plan to leave one full inch of space between the soil level and the top of the pot so that the soil won't wash over the edge of the pot when you water.
8. Hold the plant in place with one hand and pour the soil evenly around the roots. A sugar or flour scoop is handy for this part of the job. If the plant is an uncomfortably prickly sort, use leather gloves to protect your hands. A rolled newspaper folded around the plant will also work well. It is best to handle the armed varieties with caution.
9. When the pot is filled with soil, take the pot in both hands and tap it gently on the potting table to settle the soil. Chopsticks work nicely to tamp the soil in among the roots. Use your thumbs to firm the soil into place, or a blunt stick if the plant is spiny. Once the plant is firmly entrenched, the potting job is done. Do not water for several days.

Top dressing. Some experts use a top dressing of pebbles or crushed rock to give their plants a neat, finished appearance and to prevent the soil surface from crusting. This also reduces the rate of evaporation, which means that the soil remains moist longer—and that raises a question. There are two schools of thought on the use of top dressings. Some experts claim that it can cover up a watering problem—too much or too little—and that the top dressing makes it harder to check on the state of the soil. In cool, moist climates it may help to keep the soil damp enough to encourage root rot.

The opposite point of view is that top dressing prevents the soil from being splashed on the plant, allows water to penetrate slowly and evenly, keeps the soil from crusting over, and looks attractive.

There are advantages and disadvantages to both methods; the important point is to be aware of the way in which a top dressing influences the cultural techniques. Plants with top dressing will dry out more slowly and therefore need watering less often than those without top dressing. Plants without top dressing will dry out faster and need watering more frequently. Whichever way you choose, modify your watering habits accordingly.

Once the potting is finished, put your plant in a shady, protected spot without direct sun for a few days. It will need some time to adjust, and you will need some time to observe how well it took the transplanting. If the plant looks healthy and well adjusted at the end of a week, water it and put it with the rest of your plants. If the plant is to go into full sun, make the transition over a period of several days, moving it into a brighter position every couple of days—don't go from shade to sun too quickly. (This is a warm-weather caution; winter sun is rarely a problem.)

It probably took you longer to read these instructions than it will take you to pot up plants, and if you follow the steps, you'll have sturdy, attractive specimens to show for your time.

Watering

Once your new plant is comfortably situated in a new pot and the proper soil, it's time to learn about watering.

The beginner always asks, "How often should I water?" Any horticulturalist will give the infuriating, frustrating, and only accurate answer: "It depends on the growing conditions."

Quite simply, all plants require both water and air around their roots. Too much water and they drown; too much air and they starve (dehydrate). By reviewing the following seven categories—weather, light, leaves, stems, roots, containers, and top dressings—you should be able to determine your own growing conditions and the water requirements for your individual plants.

Weather. If the weather is cool, moist, foggy or overcast, don't water. The combination of moisture and low temperature means almost certain death. Succulents rot easily under cool, damp conditions.

Hot weather and wind cause the plant to use up water in transpiration, and they also dry out the soil. Some succulents have developed their own defenses against heat and drying winds, such as the coarse, heavy hairs of *Cephalocereus senilis*, or the abundant spines of *Cleistocactus strausii*, or the ground-hugging habit of *Adromischus*. In general, if the plant is looking plump and juicy, don't water it. Succulents are one of the few things to which the phrase "fat and happy" really applies—if they're fat, they're happy. When new growth is visible, then you can encourage it with a little more watering.

Light. The higher the light intensity (and the accompanying heat), the more water the plant can use. There is a greater loss of water from both transpiration and evaporation.

Plants in full sun need more water than do plants in light shade. However, it is important to note that not all succulents prefer full sun; many species will sunscald or dehydrate in direct sun.

Even those that do well in full sun need to make the transition slowly if they have previously been grown in some shade or indoors.

Some plants will develop a reddish coloration in full sun, rather like a human tan. If the plant looks shriveled or limp in hot weather, water it.

Leaves. Thick leaves and stems serve to store water for rainless periods. A thick, leathery skin on the leaf surface helps limit the amount of water loss from transpiration. Spines and hairs also help reduce the amount of evaporation and provide cooling shade.

The more leaves or the larger the leaves the plant has, the greater the water loss in hot or windy weather. If your plant has many thin leaves, it will require more frequent watering than a plant that has no leaves and is covered with long, coarse hairs.

While this does not tell you exactly when or precisely how much to water your plant, it will give you an idea of how to group plants with similar watering needs as your collection grows.

Stems. The size and texture of the stems indicate whether the stems are capable of storing moisture and how vulnerable they are to the desiccating effects of dryness, heat, and wind.

Some succulents are little more than stems; their leaves have become modified into hairs or spines (this includes many cacti and euphorbias).

Jatropha cathartica preserves water in its large trunk base.

Others have a thin, leathery covering (such as *Crassula arborescens*) that reduces moisture loss from the stem. In general, the thicker and juicier the stem, the greater its capacity for storing moisture.

Jatropha cathartica has a large, round trunk base just above the soil surface that acts as a water tank. Its way of preventing water loss from its thin leaves is to drop both leaves and stems very soon after flowering and fruiting in summer, remaining entirely dormant until the following spring. The swollen, bulbous portion of the trunk that remains exposed to wind and weather has a hard, barklike surface that allows little moisture to escape.

Roots. Plants with bulbous, coarse roots, like those of *Trichodiadema bulbosum*, have a large water-storing capacity. In addition to having bulbous roots that efficiently store moisture, *T. bulbosum* also has a tough outer covering over its roots and stems, which aids in water retention. Its small fat leaves, though numerous, are covered with tiny hairs that are an added protection against excessive evaporation from the leaf surface.

Containers. The amount of moisture lost from the soil due to evaporation is determined to a large extent by the kind of container used.

Top: Top dressing greatly lessens evaporation from the soil's surface of succulents in clay pots.

Above: White pebbles serve as top dressing in cactus containers.

Porous containers, such as common terra-cotta or red clay pots, allow water to evaporate through their sides, causing the soil in them to dry out faster than the soil in nonporous containers.

Nonporous containers, such as plastic, ceramic, or glazed pots, do not allow the evaporation of water through their sides, so the soil in them remains moist considerably longer.

Clay pots allow for better aeration of the soil but need more frequent watering. Nonporous pots require watering less often but require careful attention; the combination of wet soil and low temperatures permits the growth of fungi that cause succulents to rot. Both types of pots have their advantages and disadvantages; the important point is that each requires a different approach to growing succulents.

Top dressing. Both in the ground and in containers, soil-surface evaporation can be reduced considerably by the use of a top dressing of pebbles, coarse gravel, or crushed rock.

A rule of thumb. By considering these seven factors, you can determine reasonably well how often and how much to water your plants. If you still are not sure, insert your finger into the soil to a depth of 1 inch, or use a slim stick such as a toothpick or the thin end of a chopstick. If the soil is dry 1 inch below the surface, water it. In general, water after the soil has been allowed to dry out. As always, there are exceptions to every rule. Consult the charts on pages 32 and 33 for each species' requirements. But keep in mind that plants need more water during their active growing seasons.

How to water. How the water is applied is also important. The best way to water landscape plantings is by slow irrigation. The best way to water succulents in pots is to plunge them to the rim in a bucket of water and immerse them until the soil stops bubbling. The bubbles are from the air that is pushed to the surface of the soil as the water fills the air pockets in the soil. When the soil is saturated, set the pot on a wire rack or a bed of crushed rock or gravel to drain thoroughly. Don't set the pot in a saucer—the water may collect, and succulents don't like to sit in puddles. So put them somewhere where the water can drain off freely.

As a general rule, overhead sprinkling is not a good way to water succulents. Excess moisture might remain on the plant, exposing it to rot and other forms of fungus. Regular overhead watering can remove the bloom (powder) that is an attractive feature of many succulents as well as a natural protection against excessive light absorption. The chemical salts present in many water sources can also cause spotting on foliage. Unfortunately, the damage is permanent, so be careful.

However, there are occasions when overhead sprinkling is beneficial. On warm summer mornings, it's a good way to rinse off dust and dirt and discourage summer pests. But take care when spraying plants that have a powdery coating: don't spray too hard—the powder is not replaced if it is disturbed. Watering on warm mornings will permit the soil to dry out a little before temperatures drop in the evening.

Most tap water in this country contains dissolved salts. As water evaporates, these chemicals can build up a concentration in the soil, especially in potted plants, and sometimes appear on the sides and rims of clay pots as crusty, white deposits. These salts can burn plant tissues, especially the delicate feeder roots.

You can use rainwater, if available. Or you can leach out your pots every third time you water. Leaching consists simply of pouring water through the soil from top to bottom and allowing it to drain at least three times. This rinses the salts out of the pores of porous pots.

The visible effects of salt burn on your plants are brown tips on the leaves. Salt burns can also damage roots and weaken the whole plant. One important warning is in order: don't use chemically softened water on any plant.

Softened water has an extremely high salt content and will damage your plants severely.

For the most part, water your plants thoroughly and then let them dry out. Water early in the day so that most of the surface water will have evaporated by the time evening temperatures begin to drop. If you use overhead sprinkling, keep plants out of direct sun until the surface droplets evaporate. Remember that moisture and cool temperatures are an open invitation to various forms of rot.

Seedlings require a different watering program until they are well established. The care of young plants grown from seed is covered in the section on propagation (starting on page 36).

As you become familiar with your plants, you will begin to recognize their needs simply by observing their general physical appearance. Succulents are wonderfully tolerant—even of novice gardeners.

You will know the nervous-novice phase has passed when someone asks you when to water and you reply, "Well, it depends on the growing conditions...."

Fertilizing and Feeding

Because succulents grow slowly, most of them don't need additional fertilizer if their soil mixture is well balanced. The exceptions are the tree-dwelling jungle succulents—*Epiphyllum*, *Rhipsalis*, or *Schlumbergera* (*Zygocactus*). These thrive on a diet of half-strength liquid fertilizer applied as a foliage spray very early in the day. This application can be repeated every two weeks during the active growing period. Never apply fertilizer when a plant is dormant or resting.

When a plant is ready for repotting—the roots have filled the pot and the soil is depleted—it's a good time for very light feeding. Actually, new soil is the best way to fertilize most succulent plants; but some experts also feed their plants at repotting time, using the following methods. Some gardeners simply water the plant thoroughly a week or two after repotting and then apply a liquid fertilizer at half strength. One experienced grower adds bone meal to the soil mix at the rate of 1 teaspoonful to each 6-inch pot. Because this fertilizer breaks down over a very long time and releases its nutrients to the plant very slowly, it is, he feels, the only one that's safe for cacti. Stronger feeding can promote weak, soft growth that is vulnerable to pests and diseases; slow, sturdy growth is healthier.

In landscape plantings, another expert uses about 4 pounds of bone meal for every 100 square feet of soil. He digs it into the soil at the time of planting.

Another successful grower soaks a pound of cottonseed meal in 5 gallons of water for a period of 24 hours, then skims off the clear liquid at the top and uses it to water those container plants that are not to be repotted at that time. This is a regular spring ritual, along with any necessary repotting chores. He also uses the liquid as a foliar spray for his schlumbergeras.

Whatever method the experts use to feed their plants, they all observe these five rules:

1. Never feed a plant during dormancy.
2. Never feed a sick plant.
3. Never feed a plant that is not rooted.
4. Never feed a plant that has just been repotted. (Incorporating bone meal into the soil mix is the one exception.)
5. Always water a plant before fertilizing, even when applying a liquid fertilizer.

Landscape plantings to which no new soil is added can be fed with a commercial liquid fertilizer diluted to half strength recommended on the label. If leaf mold is available, mix in a little bone meal with the leaf mold in a 1 to 30 ratio and use it as a mulch.

Guide to Growing Cacti and Succulents

NAME OF PLANT AND MINIMUM TEMPERATURE TOLERANCE	SOIL MIX			LIGHT REQUIREMENT				HUMIDITY TOLERANCE				WATER REQUIREMENTS			EASE OF CULTURE			MOST ATTRACTIVE FEATURE		
	Gritty/lean	Gritty/rich	Rich	Direct sun	Winter direct sun	Bright	Moderate	Very dry	Average	Moist	Very moist	Dry out between waterings	Approach dryness between waterings	Keep evenly moist	Easy to grow	Moderately difficult	Very difficult	Form	Foliage	Flower
Abromeitiella (25°F.)		■				■			■				■		■			■	■	
Acanthocalycium (25°F.)		■				■			■				■		■				■	■
Adenium (40°F.)		■		■				■					■			■		■		■
Adromischus (40°F.)		■				■			■				■			■		■	■	
Aeonium (35°F.)			■			■			■				■		■			■	■	
Agave (30°F.)			■	■					■				■		■			■		
Aloe (35°F.)			■			■			■				■		■			■	■	
Anacampseros (35°F.)		■				■			■				■			■		■	■	
Ananas (35°F.)			■			■			■				■		■				■	
Aporocactus (35°F.)			■			■			■				■		■					■
Ariocarpus (30°F.)		■		■				■					■			■		■		
Asparagus (25°F.)			■			■			■					■	■				■	
Astrophytum (30°F.)		■		■				■					■			■		■		■
Aztekium (35°F.)		■				■		■					■				■	■		
Beaucarnea (35°F.)			■			■			■				■		■			■		
Bowiea (35°F.)		■					■		■			■				■		■		
Caralluma (35°F.)		■				■			■				■			■		■		■
Cephalocereus (35°F.)		■		■				■					■			■		■		
Cereus (25°F.)			■	■					■				■		■			■		
Ceropegia (35°F.)			■			■			■				■			■		■		■
Chamaecereus (25°F.)			■			■			■				■		■					■
Cissus (35°F.)		■				■			■				■		■				■	
Cleistocactus (35°F.)			■	■					■				■		■					■
Cochemiea (35°F.)		■				■			■				■			■				■
Conophytum (35°F.)		■				■		■					■			■		■		■
Copiapoa (20°F.)		■		■				■					■			■		■		
Coryphantha (35°F.)		■				■			■				■		■					■
Cotyledon (35°F.)			■			■			■				■		■			■	■	
Crassula (35°F.)			■			■			■				■		■			■	■	
Cryptanthus (40°F.)			■			■			■					■	■				■	
Cycas (35°F.)			■			■			■				■			■		■	■	
Dasylirion (35°F.)			■	■					■				■		■			■		
Dinteranthus (35°F.)	■					■		■					■			■		■		
Dioscorea (25°F.)		■				■			■				■			■		■		
Diplocyatha (25°F.)	■					■			■				■			■				■
Dolichothele (35°F.)		■				■			■				■		■					■
Dudleya (25°F.)	■					■			■				■		■			■	■	
Dyckia (25°F.)		■		■					■				■		■			■		
Echeveria (25°F.)			■			■			■				■		■			■	■	
Echinocactus (20°F.)	■			■				■					■			■		■		
Echinocereus (20°F.)	■					■			■				■		■					■
Echinopsis (25°F.)			■			■			■				■		■					■
Edithcolea (45°F.)	■					■			■				■			■				■
Epiphyllum (40°F.)			■			■			■					■	■					■
Epithelantha (25°F.)	■					■		■					■			■		■		
Escobaria (20°F.)	■					■			■				■			■				■
Espostoa (35°F.)		■		■					■				■			■		■		
Euphorbia (35°F.)			■			■			■				■		■			■		
Faucaria (35°F.)		■				■		■					■		■			■		■
Fenestraria (35°F.)	■					■		■				■				■		■		
Ferocactus (35°F.)		■		■				■					■		■			■		
Fouquieria (40°F.)		■		■					■					■		■		■		

32 / BASIC CARE AND PROPAGATION

NAME OF PLANT AND MINIMUM TEMPERATURE TOLERANCE	SOIL MIX			LIGHT REQUIREMENT				HUMIDITY TOLERANCE				WATER REQUIREMENTS			EASE OF CULTURE			MOST ATTRACTIVE FEATURE		
	Gritty/lean	Gritty/rich	Rich	Direct sun	Winter direct sun	Bright	Moderate	Very dry	Average	Moist	Very moist	Dry out between waterings	Approach dryness between waterings	Keep evenly moist	Easy to grow	Moderately difficult	Very difficult	Form	Foliage	Flower
Frailea (35°F.)		■			■				■				■		■					■
Gasteria (30°F.)			■				■		■				■		■				■	
Graptopetalum (35°F.)			■		■				■				■		■				■	
Gymnocalycium (30°F.)		■			■				■				■		■					■
Hatiora (35°F.)			■				■			■				■	■					■
Haworthia (35°F.)		■				■			■				■		■				■	
Hechtia (30°F.)		■		■				■				■			■			■		
Hoya (40°F.)			■			■			■				■		■					■
Huernia (35°F.)		■			■				■				■		■					■
Hylocereus (35°F.)			■			■			■				■		■					■
Jatropha (35°F.)	■			■				■				■				■		■		
Kalanchoe (40°F.)			■	■					■				■		■				■	
Lapidaria (35°F.)	■			■				■				■				■		■		
Lemaireocereus (35°F.)		■		■				■				■			■			■		
Leuchtenbergia (30°F.)	■				■			■				■				■		■		
Lithops (30°F.)	■			■				■				■				■		■		
Lobivia (25°F.)	■				■				■				■		■					■
Mamillopsis (20°F.)		■			■				■				■		■					■
Mammillaria (30°F.)		■			■				■				■		■					■
Melocactus (50°F.)		■			■				■				■			■		■		
Myrtillocactus (35°F.)		■		■				■				■			■			■		
Neobesseya (20°F.)		■			■				■				■			■				■
Neochilenia (25°F.)		■			■				■				■			■		■		
Neoporteria (25°F.)		■			■				■				■			■		■		
Notocactus (30°F.)		■			■				■				■		■					■
Opuntia (30°F.)		■		■				■				■			■			■		
Pachyphytum (35°F.)			■		■				■				■		■				■	
Pachypodium (50°F.)		■		■				■				■				■		■		
× Pachyveria (35°F.)			■		■				■				■		■				■	
Parodia (25°F.)		■			■				■				■		■					■
Pelargonium (30°F.)			■		■				■				■		■					■
Pelecyphora (35°F.)		■			■			■				■				■		■		
Pleiospilos (35°F.)		■		■				■				■				■		■		
Portulacaria (35°F.)			■	■					■				■		■				■	
Puya (30°F.)		■		■				■				■			■			■		■
Rebutia (25°F.)		■			■				■				■		■					■
Rhipsalis (40°F.)			■				■			■				■	■					■
Schlumbergera (40°F.)			■				■			■				■	■					■
Sedum (35°F.)		■		■					■				■		■				■	
Selinicereus (35°F.)			■			■			■				■		■					■
Sempervivum (30°F.)		■		■					■				■		■				■	
Senecio (35°F.)		■			■				■				■		■				■	
Setiechinopsis (30°F.)		■			■				■				■			■				■
Stapelia (35°F.)		■			■			■				■			■					■
Strombocactus (28°F.)		■			■			■				■				■		■		
Sulcorebutia (25°F.)		■			■				■				■		■					■
Thelocactus (25°F.)		■			■				■				■		■					■
Tillandsia (30°F.)		■				■		■				■			■				■	
Trichocereus (25°F.)		■		■				■				■			■			■		
Trichodiadema (30°F.)		■		■					■				■		■					■
Yucca (25°F.)			■	■				■				■			■			■		

Pests and Diseases

Preventing problems is nearly always easier and less time-consuming than trying to cure them. The first rule for preventing plant pests and diseases from establishing themselves in your collection is: keep the plants and planting area *clean*. Basic cleanliness eliminates the places where pests might establish themselves before settling down to feasting on your plants.

The second rule is: allow sufficient *space*. Space permits good air circulation, but the avid collector often finds this rule difficult to follow. As your interest grows, so does your collection, resulting in less and less space for potted specimens and less and less time for maintenance. So resist the temptation to acquire more plants than you can maintain in a clean, healthy environment, and your problems with pests and diseases will be few. However, if you're human like the rest of us, or if your collection is already big enough to render the foregoing advice useless, read on.

The best way to guarantee that pests don't get a foothold in your collection is to apply a systemic pesticide as part of your regular maintenance program. Systemics are absorbed directly into the plant tissues and kill any pests that try to eat the plant. Systemics can be applied as drenches, or as granules followed by watering into the soil. Some sprays also have a slight systemic or residual action.

If the pests become established before your systemic program does, here's how to deal with them, pest by pest.

Ants themselves do not damage plants, but they have an unattractive custom of bringing other creatures—aphids and scale—that do cause serious damage. Ants transport aphids and scale to convenient plants where the pests are established as colonies. The ants then return to collect a secretion called "honeydew" from their herds. If you eliminate ants from your collection, you will probably eliminate a lot of potential problems. Household ant sprays are fine on the surfaces around your plants but not on the plants themselves.

Aphids usually appear on new growth and on flower stalks, buds, and blossoms in the spring. Echeverias and kalanchoes are particularly vulnerable. Aphids are easy to eliminate. A spray of soapy water will do the job if there are not too many; if the infestation is heavy, use a houseplant insect spray and follow label directions. Some succulent species are very sensitive to chemical sprays; be particularly careful with crassulas, echeverias, or kalanchoes when spraying.

Mealybugs are found on the undersides of leaves, in leaf or stem axils, or the areoles on cacti. They can also become established on the roots of succulents. They are sucking insects with a waxy protective coating, and any insecticide used to kill them must penetrate that coating. Use a household insect spray registered for use on succulents. For root mealybugs, soak the soil with the insecticide solution. Follow label directions.

Red spider mites are so tiny that they are, for all practical purposes, invisible; you recognize their presence from the disfiguring effect they have on your plants. There are two ways to verify your diagnosis. One is to look carefully for the other two succulent pests—mealybugs and aphids—both of which are visible. If you can't find any, check the undersides of the foliage with a magnifying glass to see if the tiny spider mites are present. Another diagnostic method is to place a sheet of white paper under the plant and shake it gently; some of the spider mites will fall off the plant onto the white paper, where they will be much easier to see. To get rid of them, use a registered product such as Kelthane, or another specific miticide.

Snails and slugs are normally a problem only on outdoor plants and in certain areas of the country. They cause mechanical-looking damage—the leaves have holes, or the plant looks as if it had been scraped with a blunt fingernail. Use any good snail bait, and place it on a lettuce leaf near your plants. Don't put bait in your pots; it will attract snails and slugs, and there's the possibility that they'll prefer your plant to the bait. The lettuce leaf has the added advantage of being easy to pick up and discard along with the dead snails.

Rot is the one disease to which succulents are commonly susceptible. If it has spread through the plant, you will have to cut off the unaffected, healthy part and reroot it. Dust the cut surface with a fungicide registered for this use and proceed as you would normally for stem or leaf propagation. You can also graft the healthy section to a vigorous understock. (See page 39.)

If the root system has begun to rot, cut off the infected roots, dust the remaining ones with an appropriate fungicide, and repot in a fresh, sterilized potting mix. (See pages 26 and 27 for repotting instructions.) Don't water the plant for several days.

The worst damage that occurs to succulents is usually mechanical. Succulents bruise easily, and although the wound may heal, it always leaves a scar. Sometimes the scarred or broken leaf can be removed without seriously affecting the plant's appearance—for example, a broken leaf on a sedum or a crassula. On other plants, such as a barrel cactus or an *Agave victoriae-reginae*, there's nothing to do but tell yourself it adds character, and vow to put your remaining perfect specimens in a more protected place.

As a beginner, you'll find it easier to accept any underlying sense of uncertainty you may have about growing techniques if you cultivate the attitude that there is nothing you can't do, just some things you haven't done yet. If there is a general rule to follow with succulents, it's "Don't fuss—enjoy."

An indoor light unit that will hold many small specimens is useful for collectors with limited space or as a place to nurture seedlings, which respond well to indoor light culture.

Propagation

Succulents are among the easiest of all plants to propagate. This section is designed to give you the basic techniques of propagation, whether from cuttings, offsets, or seed. Propagating succulents is fun whether you do it to give plants to friends, to swap with other collectors for plants you don't have, or just to watch how they grow. One of the reasons it's fun is because it's easy; succulents are a tough and determined lot, and broken-off pieces will root even under the most unlikely circumstances.

The fastest and easiest way to multiply plants is by division. Many succulents, such as aloes and echeverias, produce offsets (small plants that cluster around the mother plant). These can be removed and rooted very simply. Stem cuttings, leaf cuttings (pieces of leaves), or leaf starts (whole leaves) all root and produce small plantlets with no elaborate equipment, no expensive supplies, and remarkably little attention. Some succulents, such as the mammillarias and kalanchoes, are so prolific that you may run out of friends, neighbors, and relatives who are willing to take them. A few succulents that do not produce offsets and don't propagate readily from cuttings can be propagated by grafting.

Rooting offsets. This is probably the simplest way to increase your collection. Mammillarias, rebutias, and echinopsis make numerous offsets. The popular peanut cactus (*Chamaecereus sylvestri*) forms many "babies" that separate easily from the parent. Once rooted, these develop quickly into mature plants.

Begin by removing the offset from the parent plant by twisting it gently away from the main stem. Allow it to dry for a few days or even weeks to callus the wound—exactly how long depends on the species and the size of the plant. It will form a thin, pale brown skin. To prevent rot, dust the exposed area with a fungicide. Dry the offset on a wire rack out of the sun, someplace where the air circulation is good. A satisfactory rack surface can be made of ¼-inch mesh hardware cloth.

When the callus is formed, plant the offset in whichever potting formula is suitable to the species: #2 will do for most (see page 25). Prepare your rooting soil in advance and moisten it slightly so that it is just slightly damp and crumbly, not sodden. Don't water for a week or two and then keep the soil barely damp and provide good air circulation and morning misting.

If you do not have a greenhouse or your space is limited, you can construct a simple box frame out of a dozen pieces of redwood lath. Cover the frame (the top and all four sides) with clear sheet plastic (even plastic wrap will do in a pinch). Punch a few holes in the top and sides for ventilation, and you've got a mini-greenhouse. Place this over the new starts in the evening, but remove it the following afternoon to give the foliage time to dry out before temperatures drop in the evening. Keep your rooting project out of direct sun, especially with the mini-greenhouse.

After two or three weeks, you can reduce the amount of time the offsets spend in the "nursery" and increase the amount of moisture in the soil. By the end of four or five weeks they can be left uncovered completely. A constant temperature of 70° to 75°F. (22° to 24°C.) is ideal for quick rooting. To find out if they've begun to root, give each plantlet a *very gentle* tug—slight resistance means it's rooting. Once they've rooted, make the transition into brighter light by degrees over a period of a week. Check the cultural chart for the correct amount of light for the species you're propagating.

Stem cuttings. These provide the easiest way to propagate plants that don't produce offsets. You will need a very sharp blade—a pruning knife, a razor, or pruning shears—and a sterilizing solution such as diluted bleach or rubbing alcohol. If possible, take a narrow stem. The younger shoots on a shrubby succulent or the smaller, thinner stems (the body) of a cactus are best. The smaller the surface of the cut, the less time it takes to callus. Dust

A collar of offsets surrounds a *Mammillaria elongata*; each offset can be rooted to begin a new plant.

the cut surface lightly with rooting hormone or fungicide to prevent rot. It's handy to keep around a small, soft, nylon paint brush to apply whatever preparation you use. Follow the same procedure for drying (callusing) and rooting as for offsets. Most thick-stemmed cacti and euphorbias require about two weeks to callus. The thin-stemmed types and the jungle species need only five to ten days, depending on the weather. All types callus faster in warm, dry weather and take longer in cool, damp weather.

Be sure not to let them dry out too much. Left too long, the thin-stemmed species, such as the epiphytic cacti, could dry out entirely. The main purpose is to expose the cut to warm, dry, circulating air.

Most species will root well in #2 potting soil (regular formula). The jungle species (epiphytic cacti) will do best in #3 potting soil (extra rich).

If you find yourself working with a species that is more prone to rot than root, horticultural pumice works well, according to several experts. Some use it for rooting plants collected in the wild, which often have difficulty adjusting to domestication. Others use it for rare and valuable species that are difficult to propagate.

If you have difficulty finding pumice, check with specialist nurseries, or try writing to the distributor, American Pumice Products, Inc., at the address given under "Mail-Order Sources" at the end of this book.

Leaf cuttings. These are as easy to propagate as stem cuttings for many species, such as the kalanchoes and sansevierias. Make clean cuts and follow the same drying procedures used for offsets and stem cuttings.

When drying leaf cuttings, be sure to note which side is the right one to root. It's usually easy to identify on the top of the leaf or the base of the leaf, but it can get tricky with the middle section. Pieces won't root if inserted in the rooting medium upside down. One easy way is to mark your drying rack "top" and "bottom" with masking tape and then arrange the leaf sections exactly as they were cut. Another is to cut a distinguishing notch in the bottom end of your leaf section as you are making your cuttings.

Rosette-type succulents can be propagated from leaf starts.

It generally takes no more than 2 to 5 days for leaf sections to callus, depending on the size and succulence of the plant—the thick, juicy ones usually take longest. Once callused, they should be pressed firmly into the appropriate rooting medium for that species. Follow the same procedure as with offsets and stem cuttings. The cuttings will form roots—how long it takes depends on the species—and after the leaf section is rooted, a new plantlet will appear at the base of the cutting.

Leaf starts. Leaves of aeonium, sempervivum, adromischus, and many other rosette types will not propagate by leaf sections, but will reproduce from whole leaves removed from the base of the parent plant. Look for the biggest, fattest leaf you can find and gently twist it off. Be sure to remove the entire leaf, including the leaf base, otherwise it won't always root. Allow it to dry 2 or 3 days on a wire rack before putting it in the rooting medium. Insert the lower third of the leaf in the soil mixture—the leaf will root and a new shoot will appear. A word of caution: different species take different amounts of time to root and produce a new plantlet. Some, like *Sedum morganianum*, the donkey's-tail, root easily and quickly; just tuck the base of the jellybeanlike leaves into the soil, barely covering them. Others, such as *Hoya carnosa*, take much longer. Hoyas root much more readily from stem cuttings, so that it seems a waste of time to try to propagate them from leaf cuttings.

Cuttings and offsets can be started in community containers—that is, several cuttings of the same plant in one pot or flat. Or they can be started individually in small plastic pots. These are preferable to clay ones because they help keep the soil evenly moist longer.

Plants started by any of the above methods—offsets, stem cuttings, leaf cuttings, and leaf starts—all produce plants identical to the parent plant. If

Starting succulents from seed, although time-consuming, allows the gardener to observe all stages of growth.

you have a specimen with some especially attractive characteristic, asexual vegetative reproduction (cloning) is the only certain way of propagating the plant and retaining that characteristic. Seeds, in accordance with the laws of genetics, take characteristics from both parent plants, and resulting seedlings are rarely identical to either.

Propagation from seed. This is not difficult for most species of cacti and other succulents. You generally get many more plants, but the time from germination to maturity can often be several years. Some cactus seeds may take more than a year to germinate, and then growth of the seedling can be very slow. The stages in between are absorbing, though, and if you have grown anything from seed before, you know it's half the fun of growing plants. Forget about how long it will be until you have a flowering specimen—there's a vast amount to be seen from the first thrust of life to a sturdy young plant.

Start with fresh viable seed. If the seed is old, germination can take a long time or may not take place at all. With older seed you must be very patient.

Your supplies and tools should all be sterilized, and the potting mix you use should be free of pests, diseases, and weed seeds.

A good way to start seeds is to use a plastic sandwich box or refrigerator "left-over" storage box with a fitted lid. Punch lots of holes in the bottom for drainage, including one at each corner. Put in a layer of either sponge rock, activated charcoal, or coarse granite, plus fine-grade drainage material. On top of this drainage layer pour a very lean, gritty soil mix—2 parts coarse sand and ½ part pulverized leaf mold or peat will do the job. This mix is rich enough to get seeds of any species started, and if you're dealing with plants that ordinarily require a richer medium, the seedlings can be pricked out of this mixture and potted up in richer soil after they have a bit of growth on them.

Before you put the seeds on the seed bed, press the soil lightly to make it firm and make sure that it is smooth and even across the top. Sprinkle the seeds over the surface of the soil. If the seeds are very tiny, using a fold of paper to hold them while you sprinkle will be easier than using your hands. Some experts scatter a very thin covering of sand over fine seeds; some prefer not to. Try it both ways to see which works best for you. Larger seeds should be covered with soil or sand to a depth equal to twice their diameter.

Moisten the soil by placing the container in a shallow pan of lukewarm or room-temperature water. The soil will absorb the water through the drainage holes in the bottom. When the soil begins to look moist on the surface, remove the box from the water and put the lid on the box. For the best and fastest germination, provide a constant bottom heat of 70°F.

Under natural conditions, seeds germinate in damp, sheltered places. These are usually at the base of a larger plant providing sufficient shade to keep the soil moist enough to maintain the tiny seedlings after germination. Even the driest-growing species must have moisture available during the seedling stage. At the same time, seedlings are vulnerable to a disease called damping-off, a fungus that attacks the new plant at the base.

To maintain the delicate balance between too much moisture and too little, it's essential to provide good air circulation. Remove the lid of the germinating box as soon as germination has taken place. The air circulation helps the moisture to evaporate from the soil surface, keeping excess moisture from building up.

Grafting. Grafting unites two different plants into a single one. There are two reasons for this procedure: emergency grafting saves the life of the

To graft, start with clean tools and botanically compatible plants.

Cut the scion off, making sure it's the same size or smaller than the understock.

Carefully cut off the top of the understock, protecting fingers with padding.

Place the scion, cut side down, on the understock.

Hold scion loosely in place with a rubber band around pot and plant.

The understock and the scion "donor" stand behind the new grafted plant.

Step-by-Step Grafting Procedures

A. Cut the top off understock plant.

B. Trim the understock cut to assure a flat, clean surface.

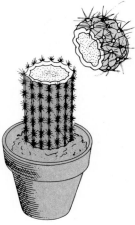

C. Place the scion cut on the understock. Make sure the thin ring of conductive tissue is matched up, or at least overlapping or touching on all parts.

D. Secure new graft with rubber band to assure good scion-to-stock contact and a successful graft.

FLAT GRAFT

CLEFT GRAFT

SIDE GRAFT

plant, and elective grafting changes the appearance of the plant or encourages better growth.

Emergency grafting is done to save a plant with a rotted root system or lower stem. It might also be necessary for rooting collected plants that do not root successfully out of their native habitat. Grafting is good for propagating a valuable plant that does not produce offsets and takes many years to mature, bloom, and set seed.

Elective or cosmetic grafting is used to change the form of the plant or to speed up propagation of stem cuttings.

The process itself consists of uniting a *scion* (stem cutting) and an *understock* (the root system) of two different, but closely related plants. The understock gives vigor and strength to the weak or slow-rooting scion. The two plants must be compatible (from the same genus or family), even though they are often of different species. You cannot graft a cactus to a crassula, but you can graft one kind of cactus to another kind of cactus. Plants should be grafted during their active period of growth and never when the understock is dormant.

The success of the graft depends on three factors: absolute cleanliness, a close fit between the growth layers of scion and understock, and maintenance of the close union of the two pieces until they have grown together. It's essential to have the scion and understock closely matched in size in order to have as much as possible of the cut surface of both in contact. Work quickly to prevent both callusing and exposure to disease. Have everything you need assembled and sterilized before you make any cuts. Use sharp tools that will make a clean, straight cut.

There are four different types of graft cuts. Which you use is determined by the size and shape of the plants you're grafting.

The flat cut. This is used for thick, globular scions and is the easiest to do. The understock must be large enough to support the scion, both at the time of grafting and as both plants mature. The scion can be smaller in diameter than the understock, but never larger. Rubber bands are the easiest way to hold flat grafts. Pass the band over the scion and under the pot on two sides.

Another technique is to insert a strong, pointed spine into both sides of the understock. Then pass the rubber band over the scion and attach it to the spines on either side of the understock. Toothpicks can also be used. Be sure that the bands are not too tight, or the scion will be injured.

Because they are flexible, rubber bands can expand with the growth of the scion. However, they typically rot away after growth begins.

The cleft cut. This is used to give a draping variety a strong upright trunk. One specialist nurseryman uses a hybrid opuntia, 'Mrs. Burbank', as the understock for a schlumbergera scion.

The side cut. This is used for upright, cylindrical plants, and is almost as easy as the flat graft.

The stab graft. This is used to unite a schlumbergera to an opuntia pad. Make a cut at the areole of the opuntia and insert the schlumbergera. It is the least common type of graft.

Until a graft has taken, avoid overhead watering; water in the cut is an open invitation to rot.

SUCCULENTS, INDOORS AND OUT

Succulents are so versatile and varied that they can be used effectively and pleasingly indoors or outdoors. They can give more interest to a landscape or decorate a living room equally well.

Because succulents are such determined survivors of nature's variations in climate and environment, they can be put to use in a number of ways—in the landscape, as portable outdoor container plants, or as houseplants. Succulents and cacti grow equally well inside a greenhouse, providing countless hours of pleasure for the collector and plant hobbiest.

Spectacular low-maintenance landscaping is easy, providing you have well-drained soil and a mild, frost-free climate like that of Southern California or Arizona. As a basic rule, succulents in the landscape cannot tolerate heavy frosts or a hard freeze. For exceptions, see "Winter-hardy succulent landscaping" on page 49.

The Versatile Succulents

Equally at home as a doorway accent, a garden border, or on a steep hillside expanse, succulents can serve as a distinctive, low-maintenance alternative in your landscape. Use your imagination when including this creative group of plants in your landscape plan. A single giant saguaro (*Carnegiea gigantea*) or *Agave americana* can provide a dramatic, sculptural focal point. An expanse of brightly colored sedum performs ably as a ground cover, while adding a mass of color equal to any bed of annuals. The photos that follow demonstrate just a few of the varied and creative ways in which succulents can be used to change and beautify the environment in and around your home.

Why are succulents so popular? Low maintenance and low water consumption are two of the more practical reasons why people switch from thirsty lawns and time-demanding annuals to succulents. Areas landscaped with succulents require only 20 percent of the water needed by equal-sized lawns. Succulents save energy, too—they don't need mowing.

Best of all, just because succulents are easy to grow and consume little water doesn't mean you have to sacrifice beauty. If you want flowers, try *Kalanchoe blossfeldiana*, with its long-lived clusters of red, orange, yellow, or salmon flowers. It's hard to improve upon the elegance of an aeonium's perfect green rosette. Some of the larger succulents, such as *Agave* or *Aloe*, or a large *Cereus* cactus, can become a striking element in the landscape.

Landscaping

Succulents can be used for all, or just parts of your garden. It's best to approach the designing of your home landscape in an organized manner. Careful planning and thinking in the early stages can eliminate wasted time, energy, and money.

To get an idea of the types of plants you like best, spend some time observing succulents growing in your neighborhood, or visit a botanic garden that includes succulents. Consider your site. What does it look like now, and how do you envision it once your planting is done? Note the

Right: Even the small crevices of a cut stone wall provide sufficient support and sustenance for *Echeveria*, *Crassula*, and *Sempervivum* species to thrive.

Below: Several varieties of *Sedum* and *Echeveria* make an attractive border.

existing structures and trees, plus the climate and light exposure. At the same time, try to decide which shapes, colors, and textures you feel would complement your landscape. In general, strive for harmony, adding just enough contrast to keep the overall scheme interesting.

Rock gardens. Perhaps you want to experiment with small groupings of succulents within your landscape. If this is the case, consider putting in a rock garden. The garden's natural textures are a perfect complement to the individual characteristics of succulents. A rock garden becomes a focal point in the landscape, providing a pleasing contrast to an expanse of green lawn. Try some *Sedum spathulifolium* and *Echeveria elegans* for low-growing plants, and perhaps some *Aeonium arboreum* to add further contrast in height and color. Other succulents recommended for rock gardens are listed on page 63.

If a cut-stone wall is beginning to show its age, or if it's too new to have any charm, planting echeverias or sempervivums in the crevices will add another texture to the wall's surface. The same stubborn determination that inspired the succulent's evolution allows it to thrive under seemingly impossible conditions.

Defining areas. Succulents are excellent plants for defining different areas of your garden. Their distinctive shapes and compact growth habits make it possible to have a neat border surrounding flower beds, edging a walkway, or acting as a clean, linear design element that unifies the landscape. When they are used as a border for water-demanding plants or a lawn, be sure that your succulents are protected from overwatering. Plant them on mounds or in very fast-draining soil.

Succulents as ground covers. One of the most widespread and varied uses of succulents is as a ground cover. If you've been wondering what to plant between some stepping stones, try *Sedum acre* (gold moss sedum), or *Sempervivum tectorum*. Both are very cold-tolerant, and their compact habit makes them perfect in small, confined spaces. Keep in mind that succulent ground covers will not stand up to foot traffic and that most require full sun.

Sedum and several varieties of ice plant serve as excellent succulent ground covers for large expanses of flat or gently rolling landscape. *Lam-*

Top: Spreading pink *Lampranthus spectabilis* adds a striking splash of color to a hillside.

Left: *Sedum rubrotinctum*, with attractive yellow flowers, can cover large expanses.

A collage of color, texture, and compact growth habits surrounds a walkway and displays the advantages of a succulent landscape.

pranthus spectabilis (trailing ice plant), *L. filicaulis* (Redondo creeper), *Sedum lineare*, and *Sedum album* are among the most effective in providing quick, even, attractive cover.

Succulents work equally well on steep slopes. *Drosanthemum floribundum*, a fast, easy grower, has spectacular pink blooms and will cling to the steepest slope or drape beautifully down walls. Succulent ground covers have yet another advantage when used on steep slopes—they help to prevent erosion.

Succulent ground covers are easy to plant. Because they root so quickly and develop rapidly, it is possible to achieve a nearly full cover within a single growing season in a warm climate. Because succulent ground covers tend to be a bit more expensive than many others, you might find it more economical to place starter plants 16 inches apart, rather than the commonly recommended 12-inch centers. Once the plants are established (approximately one month after being set out), cuttings can be made and placed between the original plants. This will give fast, even, economical cover.

In the beginning, there may be a problem with weeds. If so, you have the option of pulling them by hand or using a chemical weed killer. Once the cover is complete, weed problems should be minimal. Ice plant is especially good at strangling any weeds that stray into its path.

Easy Maintenance Gardening

Your succulent landscape, including rock gardens, ground covers, and borders, requires relatively little care, especially if you make some special preparations. Most experts say that succulents will grow in almost any soil, except those high in clay or adobe. Still, good drainage is important for the most successful succulent culture.

Drainage can be improved in a number of ways. If you already have good soil, using mounds or slopes for your succulent beds will improve drainage. It is also possible to work additional drainage material into the soil. Coarse builder's sand, sponge rock, or pumice may be used for this purpose.

Cacti (except for tropical epiphyllums and related species) generally do need more drainage than do other succulents. Be generous with the sand or small, coarse gravel when preparing soil for cacti. At the same time, keep in mind that cacti do not grow in sand alone. Like other plants, they need the nutrients supplied by organic matter in the soil.

If it seems likely that your succulents will receive more water than they need (for example, if they border a lawn), be sure to add extra drainage material, and control the amount of water near the succulents by using mounds or slopes to direct the water toward the thirsty plants, and away from the succulents.

Your cacti and other succulents will require more water during their active spring and summer growing seasons than in winter, when dormancy sets in. Water requirements will depend upon sun exposure and temperatures. Let experience and careful observation be your guide. The natural dormancy that occurs during winter, with the drop in temperature and shortening of days, reduces your plants' water requirements drastically. Give them just enough to keep them from shriveling.

The same seasonal variance holds true for fertilization requirements. Give your succulents light, regular feedings during their active growing season, and none during winter dormancy.

Sun-loving succulents that are grown in partial shade may need periodic trimming to maintain compactness of growth. Plants that have received a bit too much water and fertilizer may show similar lanky growth habits. When this happens, just clip off the young growth and set it in the ground. Succulents root quickly and easily.

Where succulents are used as a border, it may be necessary to trim growth to keep a clean line. The trimmings from any of your succulents can be used to expand your succulent landscape, start indoor plants, grow in a container, and give away to friends.

The entrance to an oceanside home is brightened by blooming *Aloe* species and *Kalanchoe blossfeldiana*. Succulents have been used throughout the landscape of this California home. (See also page 48.)

Right: A variety of succulents, rocks, and shells combine naturally in a hillside rock garden leading down to a terraced patio overlooking the beach.

Below: Succulents in containers grace the seaside patio, remaining consistent with the rest of the landscape, which is planted completely in succulents.

A totally succulent garden. The photos on this page and page 47 show several uses of succulents in one landscape. Located adjacent to the Pacific Ocean in Carlsbad, California, its owners have taken full advantage of the mild climate and the availability of diverse succulent plant material in designing this unique landscape. The front yard is a spectacular mass of bloom and color. In the back, a hillside leading down to the beach has been transformed into a huge, easy-to-care-for rock garden. Succulents are also used in containers as a means of integrating the living areas with the surrounding landscape.

Winter-hardy succulent landscaping. Even if you live in a cold-winter climate, it is possible to grow cacti and other succulents outdoors all year round. A surprising number of succulent plants are native to cold regions, including the Rocky Mountains, Peruvian Andes, and Swiss Alps. Although this group of plants does not include most of the varieties you might think of as cacti and succulents, these winter-hardy plants still have unique forms, structures, and an ability to adapt to the elements.

Three genera of plants with many cold-resistant species are *Opuntia*, *Sedum*, and *Sempervivum*. With proper care, the species listed on page 63 will withstand the cold weather in any part of the United States.

Ben Haines, a Kansas grower who specializes in cacti and succulents tolerant of cold weather, recommends that cultural practices be modified to suit the geographic location, amount of rain or snowfall, and minimum temperatures. As a general rule, he plants his super-hardy succulents in a very fast-draining soil that includes 9 parts of gravel and sand mixed together to 1 part of soil and peat, mixed.

Wherever moisture and humidity stay relatively low, as they do in Kan-

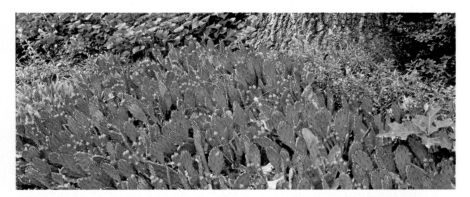

Top: This healthy bed of *Opuntia compressa* grows in New York. Its only winter protection is the shelter provided by the large tree above it.

Center: Several varieties of *Sempervivum* thrive without winter protection in New England.

Left: A fiberglass cold frame outside a New Jersey greenhouse shelters a bed of *Agave* and *Sansevieria* species from winter ice and cold.

sas, Mr. Haines simply plants his succulents on mounds of this soil mix and leaves them exposed to the wind and weather. The mounds help to accelerate the drainage, while exposure to the wind reduces the moisture content of the surrounding soil.

In areas where precipitation is heavy and winter temperatures are quite low, as in most of the Northeast, Mr. Haines recommends using a cold frame and the fast-draining soil mix. The cold frame keeps rain and snow off the succulents.

One gardener in New Jersey uses a cold frame to protect a bed of tender agave from the winter cold and snow. The frame comes apart easily in the summer to expose a bed of exotic plants.

With some preparation and determination, you can grow many succulents in an inhospitable climate, but chances of success are improved by using only those that are really suitable for cold-winter areas. Keep in mind that succulents planted outside will have long periods of dormancy, and, consequently, slow development.

Succulents grown outdoors during the cold winter months, whether protected or not, should not be watered. Frozen water around their root systems can be disastrous. Their natural dormancy in cold weather will eliminate the need for water.

A Greenhouse Garden

No matter where you live, you can enjoy a succulent landscape year-round if it has been completely enclosed. The accompanying photos illustrate an oasis of sunshine, warmth, and lush growth surviving the midwinter cold on Long Island, NY.

This greenhouse was designed by Louise Lippold when she ran out of available windowsill space for her expanding succulent collection. Faced

The variety and abundance of plant life in this enclosed landscape gives a feeling of being outdoors.

with a decision of reducing her collection (unthinkable) or expanding her growing space, Mrs. Lippold came up with the perfect combination of natural landscape and specialized greenhouse.

She glassed in a south-facing patio and side yard that was visible from the living room, dining room, and kitchen. Transformed into a breathtaking landscape, the area has become the focal point of the house.

Her succulent collection is planted directly in the ground, and covered with a top dressing of pea gravel. The sculptured mounds serve to accentuate the feeling of a natural landscape, with plants grouped according to their native origins—Baja California and other parts of Mexico, South Africa, and South America.

Left: The naturalized landscape includes collections from the Southwest desert and South Africa. Plants are grouped according to their native origins.

Below left: The enclosed succulent landscape offers a spectactular view from the Lippold living room.

Below: When plants are grown under ideal conditions, they can develop into full-size landscape specimens.

Inside the Ritzfields' greenhouse, succulents are grown in every available space.

Caring for this succulent collection is a relatively simple task. The soil was prepared to be rich and porous, and watering is done with a garden hose. The ideal growth conditions these plants enjoy have caused them to develop rapidly. No longer confined to pots or restricted in their access to nutrients and water, they have really "taken off"—in several instances, to Mrs. Lippold's surprise, even outgrowing the space originally allotted.

A standard greenhouse provides a more traditional answer to the problem of growing cacti and succulents in unfriendly climates. And the "standard" greenhouse comes in a wide variety of sizes and shapes.

For small-scale growers, there are window extension units. These are available in plastic or glass versions. Larger greenhouses could be old-fashioned, sun-heated pit greenhouses (great for conserving energy), prefab units of glass or fiberglass, or even a futuristic geodesic dome model. The price range is almost as varied as the designs, providing something for all budgets.

If you are considering a greenhouse, be sure to plan its placement carefully. Put it near your house so you can get to it easily. Greenhouses are best oriented toward the south—if you can manage it—to receive maximum benefit from the sun's warming rays. East is second best, then west; avoid the north.

Evaluate the amount of space you'll need—how big is your present collection, and how much do you expect it will grow in the coming years? Realistically consider how many plants you will be able to care for, keeping in mind the amount of free time you plan on spending for gardening upkeep. A word of warning: a greenhouse fills up *very* quickly, and it is much easier and more fun to work inside an uncrowded greenhouse. Be sure to allow enough room for all your activities: repotting, propagating, growing large specimens, and storing soils, chemicals, and pots.

If you are planning to include water-demanding plants in your greenhouse, be sure to allow enough room to effectively separate your dry-growing succulents and cacti from tropical plants—they need different climates.

A kitchen window greenhouse is the perfect place to house a small succulent collection. It also improves the view while you are doing daily chores.

A southern California greenhouse supplies a place to organize and propagate a collection and offers shelter from the sun and an occasional frost.

Some expert advice. Many good tips on greenhouse planning and management can be taken from the experience of Harold and Miriam Ritzfield, active members of the New Jersey Cactus and Succulent Society. They installed their 10- by 20-foot greenhouse in what was originally a passageway in a conservatory. As their collection steadily expanded over the years, it became necessary to expand the greenhouse. They more than doubled its size by adding another 10- by 20-foot house, with a potting and storage area between the two greenhouse sections. The original area is now used for cacti, while the addition exclusively houses other succulents.

As might be expected, their collection has kept on growing; at last count, it was estimated to be somewhere between 3,000 and 4,000 plants, mostly in 4-inch pots. The Ritzfields try to keep their plants small by confining them to little pots. As collectors, they prefer to have as many different varieties as possible within the limited space available.

They take maximum advantage of the portability of their containerized collection. As soon as warm weather arrives in the spring, the Ritzfields carry many of their plants out into the surrounding yard. This helps to reduce crowding in the greenhouse and the time that must be spent on caring for the plants. The Ritzfields have found that spring and summer rains almost eliminate the need for extra watering.

Controlling your greenhouse climate. The need for climate controls will depend upon your geographic location, the type of greenhouse you have chosen, and the plants you are going to grow. If heating in the winter proves to be financially impractical, consider a pit greenhouse and grow plants that will tolerate low temperatures. Check the minimum temperature tolerances of specific plants in the cultural charts, pages 32 and 33.

During the coldest months of the winter, most greenhouses will require some heating. Again, use the minimum temperature tolerances of your plants as a guide. A greenhouse doesn't have to be a hothouse. Plants benefit from day-to-night changes of temperature, and most will not suffer unduly if the temperature drops a few degrees below their normal tolerance for a short time. Growth may slow down, but that's no catastrophe. The

Ritzfields have experimented with various temperatures and found that a minimum of 55°F. is best for their collection. They estimate that greenhouse heating bills average around $75 per month when winters are very cold, but are quick to point out that their collection is a very important part of their lives.

The best way to evaluate the temperature of your greenhouse is to invest in a minimum-maximum thermometer. It registers the highest and lowest temperatures reached in a 24-hour period. If you know what the highest and lowest temperatures have been, you can make any necessary corrections for heating or cooling.

Good air circulation is one of the most important considerations in your climate-control planning. It is vital to the health of greenhouse plants. Damp, stagnant air is an open invitation to fungus and insect infestation. A fan will supply necessary air circulation, and is well worth the investment.

Given the nearly ideal conditions of a thoughtfully designed and well-maintained greenhouse, your succulent collection will flourish. Your plants will concentrate upon growth, coloration, and flowering, instead of survival. You'll also find propagation in a greenhouse much easier, both from cuttings and from seed. For more information on propagation, see page 36.

Succulents in Containers

Planting your succulents in containers, whether in clay pots or hanging baskets, will maximize the portability and flexibility of your collection. You can have succulents wherever you have room for potted plants: inside your home, on a patio, in an atrium, near an entranceway, or hanging from an

A collection of containerized cacti and other succulents can be enjoyed outdoors during warm weather, then moved inside for winter protection.

In this rooftop garden, landscaped exclusively with container-grown succulents, boxes, pots, and handmade ceramics can be moved and rearranged at the owner's whim.

eave or tree branch. Blooming plants can be brought indoors to bring beauty to your living quarters. A steady rotation from outdoors to indoors is possible during the spring and summer. This lets you have an ever-changing display of plants.

If you live in a cold-winter climate but still want the dramatic look of a side garden with *Echinocactus grusonii* (golden barrel cactus), or a beautiful bed of echeverias by the front door, containerized succulents are your answer.

Nonhardy succulents in containers can winter indoors or in your greenhouse. When the danger of frost is past, simply take the potted collection outdoors and sink the pots into the ground. Add a top dressing of pea gravel, and exotic cacti and succulents suddenly become a part of your landscape.

As with all other succulent culture, good drainage is essential. Be sure to dig a hole that's deep and wide enough to surround the pot with plenty of fast-draining soil.

Cacti look especially good in free-standing clay pottery. Their distinctive shapes and textures make them living pieces of movable sculpture, ready to complement your landscape or your living room.

Baskets of *Sedum morganianum* (donkey's-tail) hang from the limbs of a tree.

Miniature landscapes can be made with shallow dish gardens, or individual specimens in small pots can be grouped together. The possibilities for combining succulents and containers are endless. A number of ideas can be found in the chapter, "Developing a Collection."

Hanging succulent containers. Many succulents are well suited to hanging baskets. *Sedum morganianum* (donkey's-tail), *Senecio rowleyanus* (string-of-beads), and *Ceropegia woodii* (rosary vine) all make wonderful hanging plants because of their long, trailing growth. Hung on a patio or in a doorway, they are safe outside until frost. In winter, they do beautifully indoors as houseplants.

Epiphyllums (orchid cacti) make spectacular hanging-basket plants. Their long, spineless branches bear large, showy blooms in a wide range of colors, including white, pink, and scarlet. Because they are jungle, not desert, cacti, they require filtered shade and a soil that is rich in humus.

Above: Tropical succulents in hanging containers share an outdoor living area with pots of South African *Pelargonium* to create a pleasant corner for relaxing.

Right: A succulent collector need not include large specimens. Brick-and-board shelves serve as the display area for an entire collection in small containers.

They do well under a tree (an appropriate place for an epiphyte) or a lath overhead.

The Christmas cactus (*Schlumbergera bridgesii*, formerly known as zygocactus) and the Easter cactus (*Rhipsalidopsis gaertneri*) are similar to epiphyllums in their flat, spineless leaflike stems. They too make excellent hanging-basket subjects, offering an attractive display of colorful blooms.

Many other succulents can be planted in hanging containers. Species of *Rhipsalis*, *Sedum*, and *Echeveria*, among others, are particularly well suited to hanging displays.

Keeping plants small. If you have limited space, container-grown succulents offer more than just the convenience of portability. By keeping your collection in containers, it is possible to control the size of your plants.

If you have a giant saguaro cactus (*Carnegiea gigantea*) and you want it to remain under ceiling height so it will still fit in your greenhouse or living room, grow it in a pot. If you have a handsome *Agave americana* 'Marginata', which will grow to 8 feet in diameter and bloom and die when it reaches maturity, put it in a pot if you'd like to postpone its demise and keep it down to a reasonable size.

Although these plants will become rootbound and stunted from remaining in a small pot, this doesn't present any serious problems. Just be sure to give them adequate water and light, and frequent feedings to maintain their health.

Container culture. Container culture with succulents is easy. Your plants will need a fast-draining soil that is still rich in nutrients. Because the plants are limited in their access to food and moisture, they require more water and light and more frequent applications of fertilizer during spring and summer than do succulents planted in the ground. For the needs of specific plants, consult the charts on pages 32 and 33.

Succulents Indoors

The ever-adaptable succulent, at home in the landscape or in a container, is equally able to thrive indoors. This ability to grow under such a wide variety of circumstances is good news for all kinds of gardeners. The succulent's adaptability to an indoor climate makes it possible for everyone—especially apartment dwellers—to enjoy growing cacti and other succulents.

Succulents can add beauty to any room. Their textures, colors, and forms add interest to this kitchen corner.

Above: A sunny, south-facing window houses a cactus collection, creating a small indoor desert.

Opposite: The scarlet flowers of *Kalanchoe blossfeldiana*, known as flaming Katy, provide a welcoming bright spot in an entryway. This sturdy succulent thrives in bright light.

The uses for succulents in the interior landscape are as varied and creative as the plants themselves. If you have a collection that is still young and small, it can be easily accommodated on one or more windowsills. A row of cacti in the window over the kitchen sink can do a lot to improve the view—and your attitude—while you are washing the dishes.

When your collection expands beyond the available windowsills, simply go vertical and install a row of narrow shelves in the window frame. Because many succulents tend to stay small or grow slowly, and because many can be purchased as miniature-growing species (certain species of *Rebutia*, *Mammillaria*, and *Frailea*, for instance), they are ideally suited to growing in limited spaces.

A desert in your living room. Larger specimens can be used in a variety of ways in your interior landscape. Just as pots of cacti can be sunk into the ground outdoors to give the feeling of a permanent, natural landscape, so can containerized succulents be used to simulate an interior desertscape.

A simple plywood box, painted and lined with heavy plastic film, can accommodate your succulent collection. An inch or two of pebbles in the bottom of the box will provide sufficient drainage. Surrounding the pots with a porous material—potting soil, perlite, or vermiculite—and adding a layer of builder's sand or pea gravel as a top dressing will give it the finishing touch. The pots are easily removed for deep watering; allow the bulk of the water to drain off before replacing the pots in the landscape box. If you want to water the plants without removing them from the planter box, be careful not to overwater. This box design makes indoor landscaping a convenient reality, and advances your collection beyond the status of ordinary houseplants.

Succulent sculpture. Because succulents, especially cacti, are such structurally dramatic plants, they can be used as living sculpture throughout your home. There's something special about a tall, slender cactus that stands sentinel in a corner, or is grouped with other succulents to provide a striking accent for a room's decor.

Be sure to keep this architectural quality in mind when shopping for succulents and cacti that will grow inside your home. Because their shapes are so distinctive, it's important to consider whether the plants will suit the existing space and furnishings.

Decorating with succulents. If you are looking for an unusual way to call attention to your home, consider decorating with succulents. Whether you fancy a look that's striking or subtle, succulents can provide it. For high drama, try stationing tall plants where they will be noticed—reflecting in long mirrors, as shown in the photograph on page 60; in front of picture windows; atop low shelves; or, as mentioned, set off as sculpture.

For a subtler effect, stress the textural nature of your plants by situating them amid other textures—woven wall hangings, for example, or ceramic pots and sculptures. Place a dish of various shells, pebbles, or even raw beans next to or around a dish planted with succulents; the earthy colors and textures will look like variations on a single theme. Or play friendly tricks on your guests—mix real stones with succulent "living stones," and let your visitors try to guess which is which.

For color, succulents offer a wide range—leaves come in blue, green, blue-green, purple-green, pink, and shades of red. The sheer size of some of the plants, especially agaves and aloes, gives you a lot of color per plant.

Best of all, these decorations require little upkeep. Add some light, if you like, water judiciously, and your plants will keep your home looking attractive without taking the starch out of you.

Stand-up mirrors provide a dramatic backdrop for large cacti specimens in an apartment living room.

Artificial Light

The amount of light your succulents receive will determine their color, size, and growth habit. Some succulents get more color in sun; others show nothing but green no matter what degree of light they get. Most tend to change their leaf size, becoming more compact in habit and much smaller with more sun and stress; conversely, they become larger, less compact, and more lush with more shading, water, and nutrients.

To some degree you can have control of such factors when you plant succulents outdoors, choosing areas that get more sun or more shade as your planting site. But indoors, it's up to you to provide the proper environment by installing that wonder of modern civilization, artificial lighting.

The light requirements are another important consideration when choosing succulents for your indoor landscape. As a general rule, most cacti and many other succulents require high light levels with some direct sun. However, there are succulents that prefer moderate amounts of light—for example, epiphyllums and many haworthias. Check the plant's specific requirements in the cultural charts (pages 32 and 33), and plan your selections and placements accordingly.

Gardening with artificial light. Artificial lighting can solve the problem of growing many plants indoors, enabling them to grow and bloom even if this light is their only source of energy.

Keep artificial lighting in mind if you find you don't have enough natural light, or if your collection begins to outgrow the well-lighted areas in your home or apartment.

Artificial lights can be used either as a supplement to existing natural light or as the sole source of light for your plants. Any type of artificial light will help a plant, even if you just turn a floor lamp on for a few hours each evening. But if a room is poorly lighted by the sun, consider specialized lighting: it can make a garden of even the dimmest room. If you find that your large specimens need a few more hours of sun each day to stay healthy, they can be helped along with an incandescent spotlight turned on in the evenings. This not only provides the plants with their needed light, but gives them prominence in your decorating scheme, affording you a chance to admire them when the sun goes down.

Artificial alone. Perhaps surrounding buildings or tall trees keep your apartment or home from getting very much sunlight. Don't give up. Two avid growers in New York City have over 3,000 plants in their apartment, and they are *all* grown under artificial lights. And if that isn't amazing enough, all 3,000 are growing in a spare bedroom!

This particular light garden, owned by Harriet and Murray Goldmintz, has evolved into one of the best in the country. Mr. Goldmintz began growing his succulents and cacti long before artificial light gardening was popular, and he has gained much valuable knowledge from his experience.

The Goldmintzes use full-spectrum Vita-Lite fluorescent tubes, placed approximately 6 inches away from the plants, and burned for 16 hours each day. Because the plants are given such regular cultural treatment, their growth is very consistent and compact.

The Goldmintzes' growing room is a perfect example of space utilization and organization. The plants are arranged around the edges of the room on adjustable brick-and-board shelving, with storage space under the shelves.

Even if you don't have an entire bedroom to give over to your collection, you can still grow an amazing number of plants in one space with the help of artificial lighting.

The most important considerations in putting together your artificial light garden are the kinds of lights you plan to use. They should be full spectrum.

More than three thousand succulent plants line the shelves of this collection grown under artificial light in a spare bedroom.

Grow-lights spotlight this collection of *Cryptanthus*, terrestrial bromeliads from Brazil.

Ordinary lamps, whether incandescent or fluorescent, do not emit all wavelengths of light that are needed by plants for healthy growth in the same proportion as sunlight.

Incandescent bulbs have the advantage of being easier to install in already existing fixtures, and can also be used as spotlights. The most common incandescent bulbs are those used every day in your home. However, they have several disadvantages. They are more expensive to burn; they do not last as long as fluorescent tubes; if used as the sole source of energy, they will not encourage complete plant growth; and the heat they give off can damage plants.

It is cheaper in the long run to invest in fluorescent light fixtures. While many kinds of plants will be perfectly happy under standard fluorescent tubes, the full-spectrum types (Vita-Lite, Grow-Lux, Wide Spectrum, and Naturescent/Optima, among other brands) will result in better plant growth. Indeed, fluorescent lamps can be viewed as the backbone of light gardening. They throw off so little heat that they can be placed very close to the plants without damaging them—as close as 1 inch, although 6 to 9 inches is more common. For flowering plants, place the lamps no further than 18 inches away. If they are the sole light source, keep them operating 10 to 18 hours a day. You can buy inexpensive timers in most hardware stores. These will keep the lights on schedule, which is especially useful when you are away from home, and, as a bonus, will discourage burglars.

There are three ways to increase fluorescent light: add more fixtures, reflect more light on the plants, or move the plants closer to the lamps.

Natural light. If you don't want to add light beyond what the sun will provide, it's a good idea to place your plants on a windowsill so they can soak up as much sun as possible. However, windowsills often tend to be narrow—too narrow to fit plants on. One way around this dilemma is to deepen the sill by attaching a wooden board. You can use angle brackets for a more permanent addition, or add four legs and make the addition self-supporting and removable. This will give your succulents access to all the light that's available. Just be sure to rotate your plants from time to time so they get the same amount of light on all sides.

Indoor Care

Whether your indoor succulents are grown in natural light or under fluorescent or incandescent bulbs, their culture is relatively easy. Fast-draining soil is all-important; so is light and frequent feedings with a good fertilizer. Container-grown succulents, especially those in small or clay pots, will require more frequent waterings than those grown in large pots or in the ground.

This variation in watering needs results partly from the relatively hot, dry environment inside most houses. While the heat and low humidity will not damage most succulents as they would a humidity-loving fern, many succulents in their natural habitat go through a period of dormancy induced by a drop in temperature.

So don't be afraid to open the window for some fresh, cool air; don't feel compelled to keep your home or apartment heated for your plants. They can take—and thrive on—some rougher treatment.

Succulents for Special Situations

As a collector, you may find that succulents are suitable for many landscape situations, both indoors and outdoors. To help you choose the appropriate genera and species, here is a list of special circumstances and recommended plants. As you read through these listings, it will become apparent that many plants are versatile enough to be suitable for several situations. Keep in mind that these selections are subjective. There are many other plants that you will find effective for your own landscaping needs.

Outdoor landscaping

All of these plants are frost-tender.

Large Landscape Specimens

Aeonium arboreum 'Atropurpureum'
Aeonium tabuliforme
Agave americana
Agave attenuata
Cereus peruvianus
Cereus peruvianus 'Monstrosus'
Dudleya brittonii
Nolina longifolia
Pachycereus pecten-aboriginum

Ground Covers

Plants followed by an asterisk (*) are recommended for steep slopes.

Drosanthemum floribundum*
Drosanthemum hispidum*
Lampranthus filicaulis
Lampranthus productus
Lampranthus spectabilis
Malephora crocea*
Malephora crocea var. purpureocrocea*
Sedum × rubrotinctum

Rock Gardens

Agave victoriae-reginae
Aloe aristata
Aloe brevifolia
Echeveria derenbergii
Echeveria × imbricata
Mammillaria geminispina
Mammillaria prolifera

Container landscaping

Container Specimens

Agave victoriae-reginae
Astrophytum myriostigma
Dudleya brittonii
Echeveria hybrids
Echinocactus grusonii
Echinocactus platyacanthus
Euphorbia flanagenii 'Cristata'
Ferocactus latispinus

Hanging-Basket Plants

Aporocactus flagelliformis
Asparagus 'Meyers'
Ceropegia woodii
Crassula 'Jade Necklace'
Epiphyllum species and hybrids
Graptopetalum paraguayense
Hoya species
Hylocereus undatus
Rhipsalis capilliformis
Schlumbergera hybrids
Sedum morganianum
Senecio herreianus
Senecio rowleyanus

Houseplants

Hanging Plants

Ceropegia woodii
Hoya species
Rhipsalis capilliformis
Senecio rowleyanus

Small-Growing Windowsill Specimens

Astrophytum asterias
Astrophytum myriostigma
Cephalocereus senilis
Epithelantha micromeris
Lithops species
Lobivia binghamiana
Mammillaria species
Pelecyphora asseliformis
Rebutia species
Schlumbergera species and hybrids

Artificial light gardens

Adromischus species
Astrophytum myriostigma
Euphorbia species—small-growing
Haworthia species
Mammillaria species

Bonsai subjects

Adenium species
Bursera species
Cycas revoluta
Fouquieria columnaris
Jatropha podagrica
Pachypodium lameri
Portulacaria afra
Trichodiadema bulbosum

Especially interesting forms

Crassula 'Moonglow'
Dinteranthus puberulus
Euphorbia obesa
Fenestraria rhopalophylla
Hatiora salicorniodes
Lapidaria margaretae
Lithops species
Melocactus species

Colorful foliage

Cotyledon ladysmithiensis
Kalanchoe tomentosa
Pachyphytum 'Blue Haze'
× Pachyveria hybrids
Senecio haworthii

Attractive and plentiful flowers

Chamaecereus hybrids
Chamaecereus sylvestri
Echeveria species and hybrids
Euphorbia milii
Gymnocalycium species
Kalanchoe blossfeldiana
Lobivia species
Mammillaria species
Pelargonium echinatum
Rebutia species
Rhipsalis species
Schlumbergera species and hybrids

Winter-hardy plants

Landscape Plants

Coryphantha vivipara
Echinocereus viridiflorus
Neobesseya missouriensis
Opuntia humifusa
Opuntia polycantha
Yucca filamentosa

Ground Covers

Sedum angelicum
Sedum brevifolium
Sedum dasyphyllum
Sedum spurium
Sempervivum hybrids and cultivars
Sempervivum tectorum

A cactus collection combines with Dracaeana deremensis to create a distinctive interior landscape.

DEVELOPING A COLLECTION

Once you start growing succulents, you'll find that you want to grow more and more of them, if only because they are so fascinating.

Walk down the aisle of any nursery that carries cacti and other succulents, and see if you can leave without buying one. They're small, they're irresistible, and you may find yourself asking, "What are a few pennies for so much fun?" It's probably the way many collectors got started.

One of the first things you may find yourself doing is seeing these plants as something other than what they actually are. Many of their common names came about because they reminded someone of something else— bishop's-cap (*Astrophytum myriostigma*), for example, on page 18, or string-of-beads (*Senecio rowleyanus*). Sometimes it takes some imagination—a hairy little cactus may remind you of a troll.

This chapter shows just a few of the possibilities that await you when you bring that first plant home. You'll find suggestions for choosing just the right container for a single plant, bringing collections of plants together in dish gardens, and handling your garden trimmings—"recycling." Also included are conversations with several collectors and information on how they've handled, propagated, displayed, and enjoyed their plants.

Finding that Special Pot

Bringing your first plant home is only part of the fun. The other part is finding the right pot. Cacti and other succulents rarely need coddling. Porous soil, good drainage, bright light, and a minimum amount of water are all they ask for. So any container you see that will hold a little soil and offer good drainage can be used with happy results.

Finding one pot in which to put one plant is relatively easy, but the dish garden involves finding a congenial collection of plants (a blend of form and color pleasing to the eye) and then combining them in a situation or container that will show them off to their best advantage. Dish garden containers vary considerably, from a cast-off garden fountain to an old basket chair, for example.

Some succulents are so prolific—*Sedum spathulifolium* or *Crassula argentea*, to name two—that you have to keep trimming them back before they take over the garden path. But instead of throwing the cuttings out, start more plants for your friends, or use them as decorations for your table or elsewhere in the home. It's amazing how long these temporary plants will last. "Temporary" can mean months, as far as succulents are concerned.

Plant puns. Succulents lend themselves with remarkable ease to a play on words—"plant puns." This terra-cotta donkey is planted with donkey's-tail (*Sedum morganianum*). The stonelike head of a woman done in clay is planted with a succulent called Medusa's-head, which resembles the snakes that supplanted the hair of Medusa in Greek mythology. The succulent is aptly named *Euphorbia caput-medusae*.

These ideas are just to start you thinking. More will come to mind as you become involved in this fascinating pastime.

Top: *Euphorbia milii*, commonly known as crown-of-thorns, makes an appropriate planting in this container.

Right: *Euphorbia caput-medusae* (Medusa's head) springs from a stone head.

Above: *Graptopetalum paraguayense*, often called ghost plant, is suited to a ceramic planter, framing the head in a pearl-gray bonnet.

The inherent spine arrangement of *Mammillaria parkinsonii* forms owl-eyes, giving the plant its common name.

What does it remind you of? On these pages you will find plants that remind you of something else, but you will also discover many more examples for yourself. As you look through catalogs or browse through nurseries, your eyes will become trained to watch for the playful possibilities of cacti and other succulents.

Often the something you see can be emphasized or played up by a special container or reinforced by its surroundings. A good example is owl-eyes (*Mammillaria parkinsonii*), whose stare is repeated by a ceramic owl.

The surprise element in succulents and cacti is largely responsible for their ability to fascinate. When mature, some are very different in shape and form from when they are young. And the amount of light in which they're grown can make a big difference in foliage color.

Succulents have evolved many strange shapes in their battle to survive. Take the rock-resembling lithops, for example, at the top of page 68. They have developed a method of protecting themselves from predators by reducing their structure to two leaves, with a coloration that allows them to blend in with their native habitat. They hug the ground, their surfaces barely uncovered, hardly distinguishable from the rocky terrain in which they live.

Many cacti and other succulents will develop strange forms in individual plants. Some horticulturalists believe that the crests on the rooster plant (see the photo page 68) may be the result of early injury—a puncture wound or knife cut—that caused the growth pattern to be altered. These oddballs can be found in almost any family of succulents, including the Cactaceae, although some families are more prone than others to producing bizarre mutations. They probably start out all right, but something happens along the way to disturb the normal growth pattern.

In addition to strange shapes, you will find occasional deviations from the color norm, with some very beautiful foliage variegations being produced.

These oddities in a species are called somatic mutations, or "sports." They will not reproduce from seed, but must be propagated vegetatively if you want more plants of the same type.

A strange plant may have perfectly normal offsets. To maintain a crest, for example, you should remove it and reroot it if the plant shows signs of reverting to its true form. Or you can remove the normal offsets to avoid reducing the crested form. It is best to go to a specialty nursery to find these special forms. On rare occasions a sharp-eyed collector can pick one up at the supermarket, spotting the beginnings of an interesting deviation that other less-knowledgeable shoppers will reject. A collector knows that it may take more growth before the true character and fascination of the strange plant will be evident.

Be Creative with Containers

Containers line the walls of nurseries and import shops. You find them in supermarkets and hardware stores. In fact, they're nearly everywhere you look. Almost everything has to go into something, and this is certainly true of plants. Consequently, this whole chapter is as much about containers as it is about plants; the two are inseparable.

Containers come in all sorts of materials: glazed and unglazed ceramic, stoneware, metalware, plastic, woven grasses, and wood. Even rocks and shells offer pockets for soil.

The important thing to remember when you choose a container for a succulent plant of any kind is that it should provide good drainage. Most containers come with a drainage hole; if it is too small, you can enlarge it with a handrasp or stickle-back drill. If the container doesn't have any drainage hole, you can make one yourself. Use an electric drill with a special bit for ceramics or glass, a standard bit for wood. And if it's not convenient

Top: The geometric structure of *Crassula* 'Moonglow' recalls a Japanese pagoda.

Above: Shaped like hot-air balloons, *Euphorbia obesa* is sometimes known as living-baseball.

Left: The cactus *Mammillaria tetracantha* circled by its offsets, sometimes called pups or chicks.

Lithops species, sometimes called living stones, are of African origin.

Above: This *Aeonium arboreum atropurpureum* 'Cristata' resembles a rooster, perhaps as a result of an early injury.

Right: Backlighting emphasizes the pink glow at the edges of the leaves of *Aeonium urbicum* in bloom.

to drill a hole, you can put a layer of gravel in the bottom of the pot, set your plant in a clay pot inside the container, and water *very carefully* so that the bottom of the pot doesn't rest in water. This method also enables you to raise the level of the plant pot to where you want it in the outer container.

The advantage of plastic, glazed ceramic, or metal is that each will allow you to cut down on watering. Such containers are especially good for growing plants if you're frequently away from home.

Choose the right pot. Your container should be large enough to give the roots of the plant a little spreading room. As a general rule, select a pot 1 or 2 inches larger than the diameter of a short or rosette succulent; or if the plant is tall, a container half as wide as the height of the plant. Size is important: a small pot dries out too rapidly; too large a pot will not dry out properly. These guidelines make choosing a pot for a special plant a little easier.

Keep the structure of the plant in mind. Does the plant look best when seen from above, or is it more interesting at eye level? Is it a tree type that would be shown to its best advantage by an architectural setting? Cascading succulents, for example, do well in hanging baskets. Good air circulation keeps them thriving, and they can be viewed from all angles.

Tillandsias can be brought up to eye level. These are members of the bromeliad family, feathery little air plants that use their roots to hold fast to a perch but live and breathe through their leaves. You'll see them on page 80.

Once you have met the guidelines for culture, you can choose your pot for humor or for esthetics. Color can enhance the foliage; line and form can

Top: Graceful trailing succulents like *Senecio herreianus* (to the left) cascade from an Oriental bamboo birdcage.

Center: Collected over the years, ceramic containers made by a former art teacher and her students are worthy of study for masterful matching of plant to pot.

Left: Newly planted cuttings from mature succulents.

enhance the structure of the plant. Look at the whole—plant and container—as a piece of sculpture. If you look at them that way, what you might consider expensive for a plant or pot could seem inexpensive for a piece of sculpture.

The planter-plant grouping in the middle photograph on page 69 is a good example of how the two elements can be matched. These pots are all handmade. You'll find many more examples of handmade pots scattered throughout the chapter. Pot-making is a rewarding art; you can make a pot to order for a special plant, or reverse the order, choosing a plant for a pot you already have. And if you don't have talent along these lines, you needn't despair. The world is full of talented potters eager to find buyers, and you'll find lots of special pots already made, especially if you haunt craft shops and craft shows.

Dish Gardens

While many succulents are natural specimens, others readily fit into a group. If you find yourself collecting more plants than you know what to do with, and containers are running short, you can group your plants quite successfully in dish gardens. Cacti and other succulents are ideal for dish

Top, left to right: Succulents grow anywhere: in a pair of worn boots; in a St. Francis planter in a shallow birdbath with a gravel layer to solve the drainage problem; or through a knothole from a planter on the other side of the fence (as with the *Sedum spathulifolium* 'Pruinosum' shown).

Bottom left: Succulents in homemade containers enhance the deck of an Oregon home.

Bottom right: A miniature hibachi holds a small collection of cacti and other succulents.

Top left: A strawberry jar holds rosettes of *Echeveria elegans*.

Top right: Tiny *Mammillaria elongata* finds a home in the drawer of an old coffee grinder.

Left: Deep maroon *Aeonium* 'Schwartzkopf', *Haworthia cuspidata*, and *Crassula* species thrive in a seven-cupped homemade pottery bowl.

Above: *Aloe suprafoliata* echoes the lines and colors of a snail planter.

Bottom left: Donkey's-tail (*Sedum morganianum*) spills down flutes of an old birdbath.

Bottom right: Succulents form the head, the beads (*Senecio rowleyanus*), and the lap (*Sedum spathulifolium*) of a roguish driftwood figure.

Right: The lap of a worn-out basket chair offers perfect drainage for a varied planting of succulents.

Below: A single-layer garden uses wood, stone, and complementary succulents.

Bottom: A gate stone of soft volcanic rock has natural planting pockets and good drainage.

Bottom right: A three-tiered fountain becomes a vertical dish garden for cacti and other succulents.

gardens because many are basically small and grow slowly. Once established, they don't outgrow the pot right away.

The important thing about dish gardens is to choose plants that like the same environment, need the same amount of watering at the same time, and show the same response to light. You can build miniature landscapes using only cacti, only succulents, or a combination of the two.

Other elements (a round flat stone, a twisted piece of driftwood) can be introduced for added interest. Combining texture and color is fun, and dish gardens offer the opportunity to use a wide variety of other materials in addition to plants. The tiered dish garden is a favorite. The photos here show the variety of saucers and other containers that can be used.

The bonsai look. This chapter also covers the use of bonsai pots for containers (see the photographs on pages 74 and top of 75). These are often more

Left: Identical terra-cotta pots, planted differently, are grouped in a lawn area.

Below: A miniature scene is created in a single-layer dish garden.

Bottom: A timely garden touch: Reddish-black *Aeonium* 'Schwartzkopf' marks the quarter hours on a sundial; *Sedum rubrotinctum* fills the hours in between.

Bottom left: A plastic dishpan is packed with *Lithops* species. They like the deep root room.

Top: A collection of bonsai succulents is displayed on a handcrafted stand copied after a Japanese bonsai stand.

Far right top: Crested *Sedum dendriodeum* in a bonsai pot is top dressed with river stones.

Far right bottom: A deep blue pot enhances the color variation in *Haworthia fasciata* 'Variegata'.

Right: This *Trichodiadema bulbosum* has been repotted several times to expose the roots and encourage gnarled growth.

expensive than ordinary pots, but sometimes the simplicity of their design is just what you need. The root conformation and growth pattern of some succulents is very reminiscent of the true bonsai. And the succulent, although relatively young, can be pinched and trimmed to suggest the same feeling as the traditional Japanese miniature. In a bonsai pot, it becomes a true work of art, not just another plant.

The pot should provide a contrast in line—a tall plant in an elongated bowl, for example. Don't worry about the length of the plant's roots; if covered with soil, they will grow as well horizontally as if they were reaching downward. Plant as you would any succulent, but then mound the soil up around the stem, and give the surface a good gravel mulch. This is important because roots dry out quickly in a shallow pot. Even with the mulch, if the pot is placed in full sun to bring out foliage color, you might have to water every day. If you trim or pinch to enhance a shape, remember that growth will frequently be stopped at this spot forever. Later, it is best to nip new and unwanted growth immediately to avoid scarring.

Watering. To water without disturbing the mulch, set the pot up to its rim in a pan of water and let it soak until the surface of the mulch is damp. Always let a "bonsai" succulent dry out a little between waterings.

Don't overwater. The thick roots of *Trichodiadema bulbosum*, shown opposite at bottom left and top right on this page, serve as a good-sized storage tank. The best way to achieve this thick stock is to avoid overwatering.

Feed infrequently, just often enough to keep the plant healthy. You don't want vigorous growth; the plant would soon outgrow its pot. To keep "bonsai" succulents indoors for any length of time, place them under a bright fluorescent light.

What to Do with the Leftovers

In case your garden someday overflows with succulents, what will you do with the leftovers? If that day should come, you may find the suggestions that appear on the next few pages helpful.

Some succulents seem to grow and spread very quickly, but this is probably just an illusion. They require so little care that you're not aware of them taking over until they are encroaching on the pavement or pushing aside neighboring plants. This is particularly true if they are planted in a spot where they catch the same amount of water that nonsucculent plants require.

Gifts and party favors. When you prune your plants, don't toss the trimmings away. They can be used in a variety of ways.

Top: This *Trichodiadema bulbosum* has been kept to a miniature size by its tiny pot.
Above: The reddish tips along the branches are spines on *Euphorbia squarrosa*.

Small baskets planted with succulent trimmings fill a large basket as a centerpiece and serve as party favors at each place setting.

Potting them up and giving them to friends is satisfying and rewarding; or, you might use them as party favors. What friend wouldn't love to leave a luncheon or a dinner party with a live plant in hand? If you run out of time, you needn't pot them up. Simply put several cuttings in an attractive container and give verbal instructions for their planting and care. Even if they never get planted, they will last a long time and provide pleasure.

Right: Glowing candles, a favorite shell, and floating succulents in an acrylic bowl create an unusual centerpiece.

Below: The tortoise and the hare: *Haworthia tessallata* is followed by *Cephalocereus senilis*.

Bottom left: Fernbark blocks at each place and as a centerpiece hold cuttings of *Aeonium haworthii* and *Echeveria pulvinata*.

Bottom right: The large clamshell holds cuttings of *Sedum rubrotinctum* and *Echeveria × imbricata*; the small ones hold *Haworthia* species.

Table decorations. Try floating cacti and succulents among candles for a dramatic centerpiece. The photograph on the opposite page (top) shows a large salad bowl filled with water to a depth of 2 inches. The candles were placed upright and attached to the bowl with florist's clay. If some of the succulents sink, don't worry—it only adds to the three-dimensional effect.

You can also use them as simple table decorations. One gardener took an attractive rectangular basket and filled it with 4-inch pots of succulents to use as a one-time centerpiece. But you can also use your trimmings, unplanted, to rim a saucer, as in the Mexican-like setting of the table in the photo at top right. It uses terra-cotta pots and saucers with a bit of yarn and leftover trimmings of *Sedum × rubrotinctum*.

Household accents. There are several ways to use trimmings to brighten up other areas of the house. *Graptopetalum paraguayense* can be stuck on the tips of skewers, interspersed with strawflowers for contrast, and arranged in a chemical flask as an instant bouquet for a guest bath. Or a conch-shell bookend, planted like the one shown at top left, can be made even more attractive if the trimmings are tucked into the opening of the shell.

Many things will begin to seem intriguing as temporary containers. You will find a large source of them around the house: plastic bottle caps from laundry-softener bottles, bulk wine bottles, men's toiletries, spray cans of all sorts, even pantyhose containers (page 79, bottom). Or you can pick up shells at the beach and perhaps find wind- and water-eroded rocks with built-in planting holes to hold a little soil and a succulent rosette.

Top left: Conch-shell bookend frames planting of *Sedum × rubrotinctum* and *S. spathulifolium*.

Top right: A Mexican-hat arrangement of pots and saucers holds garden trimmings. Small candleholder saucers repeat the theme.

Above: A bouquet of *Graptopetalum paraguayense* on skewers and colorful strawflowers brightens a bathroom corner.

Above left: Playful turtle planter collection holds a sampling of succulents.

Right: *Tillandsia* species grow in the bowls of decorative wooden spoons hanging from an oval hoop in the moist atmosphere above the kitchen sink. *Euphorbia milii* is at left.

Below: Succulents substitute beautifully for fresh flowers or bows in package wraps. The tiny planter in the foreground is a baby-food jar lid.

Tree-fern-trunk plant stakes, which come in 2 × 2-inch poles, can be cut into blocks and a hole hollowed out on one side to hold soil. In some nurseries and hardware stores that carry craft supplies, you might find tree-fern balls, like the one used in the table setting shown on page 76 (bottom left). (You may have to ask at several places; they are not too easy to find.) If you have access to large pieces of bamboo, you can take the culms, saw them just below a node, and make a tiny pot. Instead of soil, use sphagnum moss tucked inside to hold moisture and secure the plant.

Holiday decorations. Expendable cuttings and temporary containers are particularly useful for holiday decorations. The rosette-type succulents, best viewed from above, gain added sparkle from the head of a straight pin used to affix them to the box top. Notice the green of *Aeonium haworthii* and the red of *Crassula* 'Campfire', which are pinned to the Christmas tree, opposite (top left). The silvery ornaments, opposite (bottom), were made from pantyhose containers hung from yarn and filled with succulent trimmings. An electric drill was used to make three equidistant holes in the half-egg shapes. Then the yarn was threaded through the holes and knotted.

Start the wreath (opposite, top right) several months ahead of time so it will be filled in by Christmas. Soak the moss in water, wring it out, and pack it tightly into the wire frame; it will contract when it dries. Make holes in the moss with a pencil. Pick slow-growing succulents that stay small. Remove their lower leaves so that you have about 1½ inches of stem to tuck into the holes. After the wreath is planted, lay it in partial shade so the plants will root. Water well, but let it dry out between waterings. Because the moss has no nutrients, feed it once every two weeks with a weak solution of liquid fertilizer. Water it just before you bring it indoors. The wreath will last several weeks inside and longer if it gets good light during the day; mist it if the foliage seems to be drying out.

Christmas Tree

2 sides:
20½" ×
6¼" × ¼"

2 sides:
20½" × 6" × ¼"

5d nails

⅜"

Bottom:
6" × 6" × ¼"

Support:
4¼" × 1¾" × 1¾"

3d finishing nails

5d nails

Base:
4½" × 4½" × ¾"

Christmas Wreath

Wire wreath frame

Sphagnum
moss

Bird netting to
secure moss.
Fastened with
thread.

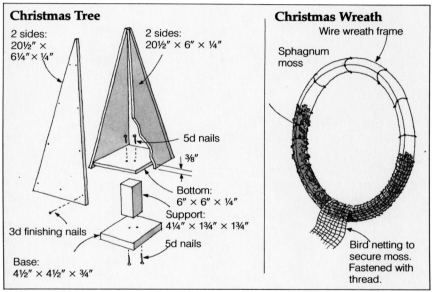

Top left: A scrap-wood tree covered with felt is trimmed with red and green succulent trimmings.

Top right: Sphagnum moss packed in a wire frame creates a base for a holiday wreath of succulents in many shades of green, accented with red berries and bow.

Left: Silvery hemispheres hold succulent trimmings hung with bright yarn on a small tree.

Top: On top of a high cabinet, hen-and-chickens (*Echeveria × imbricata*) nestles among ceramic hens for a playful touch.

Above: An easily constructed mobile of a bottle cap, fishing swivels, and embroidery hoops can be planted with your favorite succulent.

Far right: Spidery *Tillandsia schiedeana* catches prey (*T. ionantha*) in a string web woven inside a wire hoop and knotted on wire spokes.

The Importance of Perspective

Up to this point, the plants mentioned here are viewed from above—that is, you are looking down on plants that are either on the ground or in table containers. But succulents, just like many other plants, show off to advantage at eye level. By bringing them up for closer viewing, you add variety and interest to your garden landscaping. At this level, the plant and the container become more important. The donkey (page 65) stands at eye level on a terraced retaining wall; the hen-and-chicks (above) are high in a kitchen; and the Medusa's-head and ghost plant (page 66) are on pedestals in the garden.

The little tillandsias have been reserved especially for this eye-level section. These attractive, epiphytic members of the bromeliad family like to grow in an exposed situation where they can catch any atmospheric moisture and where they will enjoy good air circulation. They use their roots only to hang onto things. You can mist them, if your climate is fairly moist, or dunk them in a container of water, if you live in a dry area.

Display tillandsias in two eye-level situations, where their light, feathery appearance can be enjoyed to the fullest. They even produce small, bright flowers. You can attach them to almost any surface.

Their leaf pattern lends itself well to the twine-and-wire spider web. The little clusters of tillandsias were wrapped in place with thread. Eventually

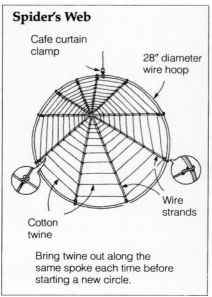

Spider's Web

Cafe curtain clamp

28" diameter wire hoop

Wire strands

Cotton twine

Bring twine out along the same spoke each time before starting a new circle.

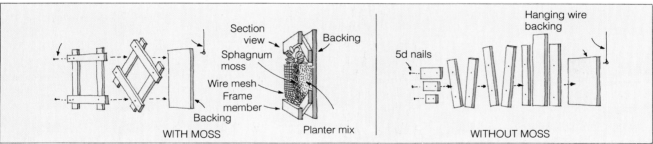

Section view — Sphagnum moss — Wire mesh — Frame member — Backing — Planter mix — Backing — Backing

Hanging wire backing

5d nails

WITH MOSS

WITHOUT MOSS

their roots will curl around the string of the spider web. On the spoon mobile (page 78), they were attached with white glue, staples, even a small nail. Eventually they will root themselves to the wooden bowls.

Originals—Containers You Can Make

Wooden planting pockets. The handsome planters shown on this page were designed by George L. Schmidt of Torrance, California, whose garden you see on page 88. Mr. Schmidt used scraps of cedar or redwood grapestake fencing.

To make your own, take even lengths of 3- or 4-inch-wide scrapwood; the length will depend on how large you want your planter to be. Those shown are about 15 × 15 inches. Determine your design by crisscrossing the lengths loosely on top of a solid wood backing in such a way as to create a planting pocket. Use galvanized nails to attach the first layer or two to your backing. At this point, turn the planter over and attach a galvanized wire hanger, winding it around a nail head.

Fill the planting pocket with a light soil mix of one-third loam, one-third peat moss, and one-third sponge rock. Then cover it with a layer of damp sphagnum moss or black plastic and stretch a piece of ½-inch wire mesh over all. Finally, nail on the balance of your strips, fill any crevices with moss, and plant as you wish. Leave the plaques horizontal for a couple of weeks until the plants root. Maintain moisture with a light spraying.

A vertical volcanic garden. To gain more display area for your plants, you might build a vertical Featherock planter like the one shown on page 82. The

In a small bedroom atrium, wooden planting pockets hold a wide variety of succulents. Note depth of planting pockets shown in detail (bottom).

Right: Featherock planter with succulent collection was constructed using common household tools.

Bottom: Before planting, the rocks were assembled over a length of galvanized pipe.

Vertical Featherock Planter

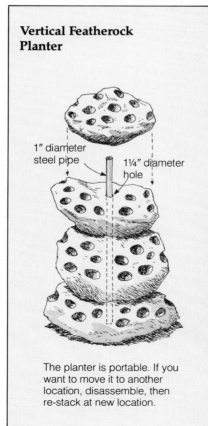

1" diameter steel pipe

1¼" diameter hole

The planter is portable. If you want to move it to another location, disassemble, then re-stack at new location.

Left: A 10-minute project: make a do-it-yourself scrap-wood easel to hold a temporary display of new acquisitions. The flat holds *Aeonium* 'Schwartzkopf'.

Below: Red, yellow-green, to blue-green —a rainbow of succulents grows in this attractive freestanding planter box made of wood scraps.

porosity of this volcanic rock makes it an ideal container for plants, particularly those requiring good drainage. It's light in weight and can be carved without requiring special tools.

This planter consists of four layered rocks, held together with a length of pipe through the center. It was designed to be portable. Presently, it fills a small area where gardening possibilities are limited. Later, it can be taken apart and moved to another location.

You can buy Featherock in building-supply outlets that sell ornamental garden rocks and landscaping materials. Choose rocks that fit together fairly well—one on top of the other—before you bring them home to build the planter. Once home, build them up again. Use a chisel to make the necessary adjustments to improve their fit. Wear gloves as you work to protect your hands, and glasses to protect your eyes.

Marking the center of each rock, disassemble the pile, and use a 1¼-inch extension bit to drill a hole down through the center of each one. The hole should be wide enough to receive a 1-inch galvanized iron pipe. Insert the pipe into the bottom rock, then assemble each rock layer onto the pipe.

Once the planter is assembled, decide where you want your plants, and begin hollowing out planting pockets. Use an electric drill to get each hole started, then expand it with a hammer and chisel. Each hole should be large enough to receive the rootball of the plant, plus a little fresh soil. On vertical rock faces, slant the hole down as much as possible so it will hold water and soil more easily.

After you finish all the holes, you are ready to plant. Start at the top and work down, rather than the other way around, to avoid spilling soil on new plantings. If needed, you can tuck sphagnum moss into the holes to help hold the soil. Water the plants thoroughly.

Collecting for the Fun of It

One thing about collectors: they always manage to find room for one more plant. Their gardens may be overflowing, but by squeezing out an inch here and an inch there, they find a spot for one more little cactus. Many have had to go vertical in their gardening.

If you find yourself cramped for space, here are a few suggestions on how you might handle the situation and still have the pleasure of more plants.

The stand shown at the top of page 83, for example, was put together in about ten minutes. The lumber pile yielded a three-board section of grape-stake fencing, plus a 2 × 2-inch pole that once was used to support a young tree. This was nailed perpendicularly to the fencing at waist height to form a shelf, backed by a weathered strip of wood of equal length. An old nursery flat was nailed above it to suggest a picture frame for an ever-changing display. It's an ideal place to set new plants when you bring them home from the nursery. At waist level, the pots are easy to water and fun to look at until you decide where you want to put them.

The stand at right, one of several in the garden of M. R. Stern, is more elaborate and more permanent. (Mrs. Stern's greenhouse is shown opposite.) Constructed of 1 × 8-inch redwood, the three lower tiers fit into notches in the uprights. The sketch below shows you how to put it together.

Mrs. Stern is a succulent collector, as you might have guessed. She estimates that she has between five and six thousand plants in her collection. She and a friend designed her greenhouse for choice, rare plants that didn't seem to do so well outdoors. The framework is redwood, the walls are double-strength glass. The roof is clear corrugated plastic with a light transmission of 95 percent; the west half of the roof and the west wall have denser fixed plastic panels allowing only 55 percent light penetration.

Inside, gravel is used under the plant benches on either side of a 3-foot-wide brick aisle. A high window at one end and the door at the other

Above: A four-tiered rack (plan at left) brings containers to a workable level and offers sun and shade to a succulent collection.

Opposite: Built on a brick foundation, this 9-by 12-foot greenhouse shelters choice plants. The building stands 6½ feet high at the eaves, 8 feet at the peak.

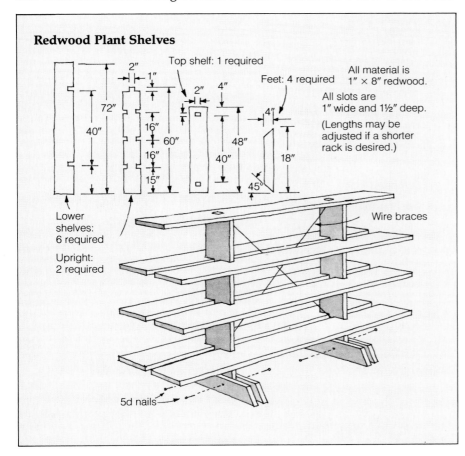

Redwood Plant Shelves

Top shelf: 1 required

Feet: 4 required

All material is 1" × 8" redwood.

All slots are 1" wide and 1½" deep.

(Lengths may be adjusted if a shorter rack is desired.)

2"
1"
72"
40"
16"
16"
15"
2"
4"
60"
48"
40"
4"
4"
18"
45°

Lower shelves: 6 required

Upright: 2 required

Wire braces

5d nails

Above: Handcrafted basket-weave ceramic planters hang from the edge of a picnic table.

Top right: A fascinating array of pots and plants fills the Trues' garden.

Right: The Trues collect for the joy of discovery of beautiful or unusual succulents and bromeliads.

provide good cross-ventilation. In summer, with both open, the temperature stays around 90 degrees; in winter, with both closed, it rarely gets below 85 degrees. Neither a heater nor a fan were necessary in the coastal climate where she lives. Her workbench stands just outside the door.

Collecting as a lifestyle. Dr. and Mrs. True, owners of the garden shown on this page, are also deeply committed collectors; she collects succulents, he collects bromeliads. Their enthusiasm and love for their plants is evident. They are both active in their local specialty garden clubs.

Left: Clothespins hold hanging pots of cacti and other succulents in place on the clothesline in the Yasuis' casual garden.

Below: An old plant stand holds more containers.

They also make their own containers as a joint endeavor. He, using the potter's wheel, makes the large ones; she makes the smaller ones by slip casting. Whenever a plant needs a pot, she opens a cabinet door and chances are the right one is there.

The Trues enjoy traveling and usually bring home plants on a permit issued by the U. S. Department of Agriculture, Plant Quarantine Division. Plants must be brought in bareroot, but succulents and bromeliads make it easy to comply.

Their advice to beginners? Join a local Cactus and Succulent Society where you can meet and exchange plants with others interested in the same subject. Club libraries provide source material and, as a part of the larger national Society, each club receives a monthly journal to keep members up to date in their fields of special interest. See page 139 for more information.

An ever-changing collection. Part of the joy of John and Annie Yasui's garden in Hawaii, seen above and at right, is its changing face. As soon as one plant moves out, another moves in. Plants are shared with friends, neighbors, and civic organizations for their bazaars. It's busy, cluttered, loved, tended, and always changing.

It's almost exclusively a container garden. Mrs. Yasui found that plants did much better in pots than in the clay soil prevalent in her garden.

Their succulents, including cacti, are just part of a collection that ranges from vegetables to roses. Anything and everything finds a home.

Mrs. Yasui can't remember when she started collecting succulents, but feels she was one of the first residents of Hawaii to order them from California. She likes to propagate and share them now.

For her succulents, she uses mostly plastic pots, which don't have to be watered so often. For soil, she mixes volcanic black sand with a little topsoil and some sponge rock, if it's available. She feeds her plants only in summer because they develop soft foliage if fed in winter.

Top: Crossbeams of a screened 8- by 12-foot area in the Schmidts' garden supports plastic panels providing 35 percent shade. Chain-link screening supports pots.

Right: Low benches around the Schmidts' garden hold succulents arranged by plant family and color.

Below: The Schmidts' interest in succulent propagation is apparent. The uniform plastic pots can be packed closely, and plants need to be watered less frequently.

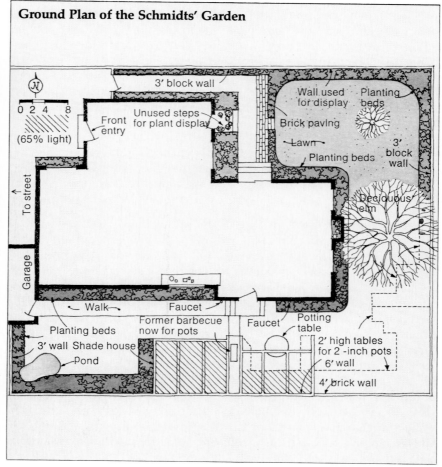

Ground Plan of the Schmidts' Garden

3' block wall

Wall used for display · Planting beds

0 2 4 8

(65% light)

Front entry

Unused steps for plant display

Brick paving

Lawn

Planting beds

3' block wall

To street

Deciduous elm

Garage

Walk

Faucet

Former barbecue now for pots

Faucet

Potting table

Planting beds

3' wall Shade house

Pond

2' high tables for 2-inch pots

6' wall

4' brick wall

A controlled collection. The gardening style of the George Schmidts in California is a direct contrast to that of the Yasuis in Hawaii. In the Schmidts' garden shown on the opposite page, plants are automatically arranged in orderly rows of color and form, as though always on display.

Mr. Schmidt is not a collector in the sense of having one of everything. But he likes his plants to be attractive; he uses them in many planting situations, and he chooses them with an eye to eventually grouping them together. Now that Mr. Schmidt has retired from the nursery business, his home garden is a natural evolution from vocation to avocation.

The Schmidts' garden is divided into separate work areas. In addition to the plant benches shown, they use a retaining wall and steps leading from the house as display areas. Plants are moved according to their requirements for shade and sun.

A plan of their garden shows how Mr. Schmidt organized it to take maximum advantage of a relatively small area. Good planning is followed up with good maintenance. This enables the Schmidts to get maximum enjoyment from their hobby.

A northern garden. The Barads live in central New Jersey, which at first would seem to be an uncongenial location for a cactus and succulent collector. A large collection of cacti and stapeliads lives most of the year in the Barad greenhouse, but an extensive outdoor rock garden is planted each spring with echeverias, aeoniums, and similar species. The plants overwinter in flats under the greenhouse benches and are planted directly into the ground of the rock garden during the summer. Other hardy species, such as those of *Sedum* and *Sempervivum*, are permanent occupants of the rockery.

Left: Springtime at the Barad home means a move of succulents from winter greenhouse to outdoor planting bed.

Below: The empty bed will be prepared for replanting. The Barad rock garden thrives in its New Jersey setting, usually considered too cold for succulents, after a greenhouse overwintering.

ENCYCLOPEDIA OF SUCCULENTS

The seemingly endless number of succulents available guarantees that you can find some that are sure to catch your fancy and suit your lifestyle.

Now that you've had a glimpse of the many plants that are classified as succulents and of all the ways in which they can be used, you're probably ready to go out and buy at least one plant, perhaps to start a collection or to increase your present one. But where do you start?

Thumb through this chapter to look at the photographs and read the plant descriptions. Which kinds of plants do you find most appealing? Which are best suited to the conditions you can provide? Evaluate the available space, light, and your own cultural expertise.

In each instance, you'll find at least one photograph of a species from each genus mentioned in the chapter, along with discussion of specific cultural needs. More detailed information can be found in the charts on pages 32 and 33.

Once you've found some likely candidates, there are several ways to buy them. The specialty nursery or mail-order specialist is your first source. As cacti and other succulents have become increasingly popular, the selection you now find in retail nurseries, plant shops, and even in supermarkets is also increasing.

Order Succulents by Mail

You'll probably find, however, that some of the most interesting or unusual plants aren't offered through retail stores, but they can be ordered by mail. Refer to the listing on pages 138 and 139 for general and specialty succulent nurseries that deal in mail-order sales.

The mail-order nurseries make it possible for collectors all over the United States and Canada to obtain a wide variety of high-quality plants. Each nursery puts out a catalog. Try writing away for a few of them.

The Cactus and Succulent Society

You can get lots of good information about plant availability and some expert cultural tips by joining a local chapter of the Cactus and Succulent Society, or by subscribing to their journal. For information, write to the national headquarters at the address given in the listing of mail-order sources on pages 138 and 139.

The journal carries advertisements for many mail-order specialty nurseries. Becoming a Society member often has another advantage—it is traditional for members to exchange cuttings of their plants with one another. It can be an excellent way to build up a varied collection at relatively little cost, and also to meet other collectors.

Name that Plant

If you have purchased an unidentified plant or been given a cutting by a neighbor or friend, you'll probably be curious about that plant's name. Knowing the name will be useful in a practical sense, as well—the scien-

A wide selection of cacti and other succulents is often available in retail nurseries.

Lemaireocereus dumortieri has prominent ribs.

A *Melocactus* species develops a cephalium.

tific name is the only reliable means of matching a plant to its cultural requirements. The index at the back lists all the plants discussed in this book by their proper scientific names. If a plant has an unlisted common name, or no name at all, paging through this gallery of photographs should help you narrow the possibilities down to one or two genera.

While many gardeners would find it easier to locate each plant by its common name, the fact is that some plants have several and others have none. Botanical nomenclature has a distinct advantage in that every known plant has a unique name, and that same name is used by horticulturists and botanists throughout the world. Because scientific names are more accurate, the genera and the species in this gallery are listed by their scientific names, in alphabetical order.

If you know a particular succulent by its common name only, please consult the list on page 140.

Using the Encyclopedia

Before looking at the encyclopedia, it might be helpful to become familiar with some of the terms used here to describe the plants. Whenever possible, complex botanical terminology has been avoided. But succulents, like any other specialized subject, require specific descriptive terms. The plant's name is one unit of that description. But there's more to botany than just a Latin name.

When you begin to read the text in the general descriptions and flower descriptions, you'll probably come across some terms that are unfamiliar. The following vocabulary list will explain some of the specialized words.

Vocabulary list

Apex. The top of the plant, the growing tip.

Areole. The soft, cushioned base of the spines on a cactus.

Axil. The joint of two plant parts, such as tubercles or stem and leaf.

Bract. Specialized leaves that are brightly colored, often mistaken for petals.

Caudex. A swollen, tuberous stem, usually above ground level.

Cephalium. A specialized growth that forms on the apex of some species of cacti after they have reached maturity. It is usually woolly and bears the flowers.

Clustering, clumping. A group of stems that grow together to form one mass.

Columnar. An upright, cylindrical-shaped stem.

Crested. An irregular growth that forms on some succulents like a cockscomb.

Depressed. A stem that is wider than it is high, often with a sunken center.

Epiphyte. A plant that grows on trees, but is not a parasite.

Glaucous. The texture of stems and foliage with a special powdery or waxy coating.

Globular. Globelike, spherical.

Hooked spines. Central spines with recurved fishhook tips.

Monotypic. A genus with only one species.

Procumbent. Stems that lie on the ground.

Ribs. Vertical ridges of a cactus stem.

Rosettes. Symmetrically arranged leaves, reminiscent of a rose.

Stapeliad. A group of plants having in common starfish-shaped flowers.

Tuber. A swollen root system.

Tubercles. Enlarged protuberances of a cactus stem.

Window. An adaptive device at the top of some succulent leaves for admitting light to the interior of the plant.

Wool. A soft, dense, hairy growth in the areoles of cacti.

×. Denotes a plant of hybrid origin.

Each genus description in the encyclopedia includes the following:

Name of genus. A group of plants within a botanical family, each sharing certain common characteristics.

Family. A large, general grouping of genera with common traits.

Group. A classification used only for cacti in this book, relating to their basic types within the family.

Origin. The plant's native habitat.

General description. The important characteristics of the genus—stems, leaves, spines, form, color, and size.

Flower description. The shape, color, size, location, and season of flowers occurring in the genus.

Propagation. The means of multiplying the plant (the first mentioned is the most common).

Culture. The recommended general procedures and any special notes.

Recommended species. A listing of the species, based on availability of the plant material, that includes: the species name, previous scientific name, and the common name or names, plus a brief description of the species' distinguishing characteristics. *Availability* gives a listing of the catalogs by number (see pages 138 and 139) offering the plant for sale at the time of the publication of this book.

Top: *Trichocereus thelegonus* crawls along the ground.

Center: *Gymnocalycium* species is distinctly tubercled.

Above: A *Lobivia* species exhibits a globular stem.

Far left: *Cereus* species have a branching, columnar form.

Left: *Mammillaria* species are generally clustering cacti.

Right: *Abromeitiella brevifolia*
Far right: *Adenium obesum*

Abromeitiella

Family: Bromeliaceae.
Origin: Argentina.
General description: All species of this genus form tightly congested clumps of individual rosette plants. Mature clumps may reach 3 to 4 feet in diameter. Tiny, sharp spines are at the tips of each leaf.
Flower description: Greenish yellow tubular flowers, measuring approximately 2 inches long, appear from the top of each leaf rosette in summer.
Propagation: Division.
Culture: General succulent culture. Easy to grow.
Recommended species: A. brevifolia. Small mounding plant. Individual rosettes are 2 to 3 inches in diameter. Available: (1), (18), (22), (31).

Acanthocalycium

Family: Cactaceae.
Group: Echinopsis.
Origin: Argentina.
General description: At maturity, an acanthocalycium measures only 4 to 5 inches in diameter and 8 inches in height. The globular plant is green to glaucous blue, with 10 to 15 ribs and horn-colored spines 1½ inches long.
Flower description: Funnelform flowers are mostly white or pink, occasionally yellow. They are 2 inches or more in length and make a showy appearance in summer at the apex of the plant.
Propagation: Seed.
Culture: General cactus culture. Needs to be kept fairly dry during winter; will tolerate some overwatering in summer.
Recommended species: A. glaucum. A glaucous blue color makes this plant attractive even when not in bloom. Flowers are yellow, spines black on columnar growth. Available: (7), (8).

Acanthocalycium glaucum

A. violaceum (Violet sea-urchin). Columnar to 8 inches tall. Lilac-colored flowers; brown spines. The most satisfactory species of the genus. Widely available.

Adenium

Family: Apocynaceae.
Origin: Socotra, tropical East Africa, South Africa.
General description: Adeniums are small, treelike plants with gnarled trunks, each one creating its own sculptural design. The base, or caudex, varies from gray to pale brown, and the stem is fleshy. Small plants catch the eye because they seem to have been molded of clay. As they get larger, they branch irregularly. Shiny, long, green leaves are attractive, though not produced in any great abundance.
Flower description: Flowers are brilliant red to pink and appear in clusters

at branch tips in summer. Funnel-shaped blooms are 2 inches or more in diameter.

Propagation: Seed, sometimes cuttings.

Culture: Keep plant underpotted in loose soil. Provide ample water and fertilizer during the growing season. A minimum temperature of 65°F. is absolutely necessary throughout the whole year. It takes many years for a plant to reach even 3 feet in height. This is a difficult plant to manage, so it is not recommended for a beginner.

Recommended species: A. obesum (Desert rose). Shrub or small tree to 15 feet in the wild, but much smaller in cultivation. Pink flowers. Native to East Africa. Available: (16), (25), (31), (33).

A. obesum subspecies *multiflorum* (often simply listed as *A. multiflorum*). Darker colored flowers. Native to South Africa. Available: (7), (9), (22), (33).

Adromischus species

Adromischus

Family: Crassulaceae.

Origin: Central to southern Africa.

General description: These stout-stalked succulent herbs or small bushes have a wide variety of interesting leaves, which sometimes form rosettes. Foliage color can range from green to grayish blue, sometimes marked with splotches of maroon or purple. Many leaves are smooth; other species have a crinkled texture that somewhat resembles a raisin, caused by small warts on the surface of the leaf. Aerial roots are sometimes produced along the stems. When dry, they resemble Spanish moss.

Flower description: Small whitish or reddish insignificant flowers are borne on short spikes from the top of the plant in summer.

Propagation: Stem and leaf cuttings.

Culture: General succulent culture. Water very lightly during winter dormancy. Plants should be exposed to sun to bring out best coloration. They do well indoors and under lights. Their short, gnarled trunks make them beautiful "bonsai" specimens.

Recommended species: A. cooperii (Plover-eggs). Light green leaves with purplish red flowers. Available: (15), (17), (22), (24).

A. cristatus (Crinkle-leaf plant). Stems covered with many red-brown aerial roots. Widely available.

A. festivus. Purplish brown spotted leaves. Widely available.

A. maculatus (Calico-hearts). Brown-spotted leaves. Available: (15), (17), (18), (22), (24), (33).

Aeonium

Family: Crassulaceae.

Origin: Canary Islands, western part of North Africa.

General description: Variety is the word for aeoniums. Some grow into large bushes; others make just one large rosette that grows to 16 inches in diameter. Leaves are usually glossy but some are covered with fine hairs. Leaf color ranges from apple green to a very dark maroon-tinged red.

Flower description: Flowers are usually yellow. They make up for their small size by their profusion, growing at the ends of long stems. The blooming season varies greatly among the various species. Each stem flowers over a long period while individual flowers come and go. They can be cut and used in arrangements, but stems with leaves are more dramatic.

Propagation: Seed, cuttings.

Culture: Very easy to grow. Although aeoniums are succulent, they need more than average water and food to grow their best. Without sufficient water they just stand still; if neglected enough, they seem to shrivel away. Full sun or partial shade suits them. Aeoniums make good landscape plants in frost-free areas. Potted specimens require large containers.

Recommended species: A. arboreum. Can become a large, spreading bush

Aeonium tabuliforme

Aeonium haworthii

with multiple branches. Glossy green rosettes. Bright yellow flowers. Leaf stems cut well and last for 2 to 3 weeks. Leaves fall from the back of the rosette after turning brown and curling. Flowers winter–spring. Widely available.

A. arboreum 'Atropurpureum'. Rosettes are dark maroon. A good accent among predominantly green plants. Widely available.

A. haworthii (Pinwheel plant). Rounded shrub of red-edged, blue-green rosettes. Flowers in spring. Widely available.

A. lindleyi. Small shrub to only 1 foot. Yellow flowers in summer. Available: (6), (7), (22), (31), (33), (36).

A. 'Schwartzkopf'. Almost black rosettes. Unusual addition to any planting. Available: (6), (7), (15), (18), (22), (31), (36).

A. tabuliforme. Low-growing, flat, green rosettes up to 16 inches in diameter. Yellow flowers in summer. Available: (6), (13), (16), (22), (35), (36).

Agave

Family: Agavaceae.

Origin: North and South America.

General description: Members of this large genus of over three hundred species grow in rosette form, ranging from mature sizes of 3 inches to 8 feet or more in diameter, depending upon the species. Stems are generally very short. The leaves of an agave are succulent, shaped like long triangles. They range in color from glaucous gray to dark green to pale apple-green, sometimes marked with white lines. Some species have hooked spines on the edges of their leaves and nearly all species have a sharp spine on the tip of the leaf.

Flower description: White to yellow-green flowers are borne on long terminal stalks that come from the center of the rosette. These bear hundreds of small bell- to tube-shaped flowers at one time. The individual agave plant flowers only once, after which it dies. Plants usually produce suckers vigorously, and the young plants eventually replace the parent plant. Flowering is dependent upon maturity.

Propagation: Offsets, bulbils formed on the flower stalk, seeds.

Culture: General succulent culture. The agave is very easy to grow, a good beginner's plant. Generally speaking, it requires a large pot and plenty of water and fertilizer during its active growing season. In frost-free areas, the large species make dramatic accents outdoors. They need little attention, but can spread to take up considerable space. Water and fertilizer speed maturity and flowering.

Recommended species: A. americana (Century plant). Gray-green rosette to 8 feet in diameter. Available: (3), (6), (13), (16), (21), (23), (33).

A. attenuata. Green to gray-green, spineless, forms trunks, and matures to landscape size. Available: (6), (13), (21), (31).

A. bracteosa. Pale or gray-green rosette has tiny marginal teeth, grows to 4 feet in diameter. Available: (6), (9), (13), (16).

Agave angustifolia 'Marginata'

Right: Agave species
Far right: *Agave victoriae-reginae*

A. parviflora. Dark green leaves with white lines on upper surfaces, matures to only 6 inches in diameter. Available: (6), (7), (15), (22), (23), (25), (36).

A. utahensis var. *nevadensis.* Glaucous green rosette that grows to a maximum of 16 inches. Available: (7), (13), (16).

A. victoriae-reginae. Very attractive. Dark green leaves with white lines on underside, grows to 12 inches. Widely available.

Aloe

Family: Liliaceae.

Origin: Drier regions of Africa, Madagascar.

General description: There is a great diversity among the plants of this genus. In overall form, they range from almost stemless plants to others that are 30 feet high. Some are rosettes of lance-shaped leaves; others are climbers, their long stems covered with dead leaves surmounted by actively growing terminal rosettes. Leaf color varies from gray to all shades of green and glaucous blue. Many species have spines on the edges of the leaves. The spines of some are sharp; those of others are short and soft. A few are spineless.

Flower description: Tubular flowers measure 1 to 1¼ inches long and are carried on spikes above the foliage, with the number of flowers per spike varying from few to many. Colors can be white-greenish to yellow, but shades of red and orange predominate among the commonly cultivated species. The flowering season varies considerably but is heaviest in autumn. Many species flower periodically throughout the year.

Propagation: Seed, offsets.

Culture: General succulent culture. On the whole, aloes are easy to grow in containers or in the ground, where weather permits. Some of the very small species are difficult to manage. In general, the key to successful culture is well-drained soil and adequate amounts of water. Some take full sun; others must have shade or filtered light. Be sure to check light requirements wherever you buy the plants.

Species well suited to containers include: *A. aristata, A. barbadensis* (commonly sold as *A. vera*), *A. humilis, A. plicatilis, A. rauhii,* and *A. variegata.*

Recommended species: A. aristata (Torch plant, lace aloe). Stemless rosettes edged with soft white teeth. Widely available.

A. barbadensis (Green aloe, burn aloe, *A. vera*). Stemless plant with green leaves. Juice of leaves effective for minor burns. Widely available.

A. brevifolia. Stemless rosettes of glaucous green leaves armed with sharp white teeth. Widely available

A. distans (Jewelled aloe). Forms dense clumps of long creeping stems. Glaucous green leaves edged with yellow teeth. Red flowers borne on 2-foot spikes. Good for growing on a fence or steep bank. Available: (13), (16), (20), (22), (24), (33).

A. ferox (Cape aloe). Long, lance-shaped leaves, green tinged red, on trunks to 6 feet high. A large plant for landscape use. Available: (13), (16), (20), (23), (24), (33).

A. humilis (Spider aloe). Stemless clumps of glaucous green leaves edged with white teeth. Available: (6), (18), (23), (25).

A. nobilis (Golden-tooth aloe). Lance-shaped, 8-inch green leaves edged with yellow teeth. A sprawling plant with stems to 6 feet. Available: (3), (13), (15), (20), (21), (23), (26).

A. plicatilis. Large, glaucous green, smooth-edged leaves on a large shrub or small tree. Opposite leaves characteristically grow in a flat plane rather than a rosette. Available: (6), (13), (23), (35), (36).

A. variegata (Tiger aloe). White-spotted, boat-shaped green leaves. Stemless. Widely available.

A. vera. (See *A. barbadensis.*)

Aloe plicatilis

Aloe nobilis

Anacampseros species

Anacampseros

Family: Portulacaceae.

Origin: South Africa.

General description: Small plants (usually under 6 inches when mature) form rosettes of leaves that are lance-shaped or almost round. Many are dark green, but there are other colors. The easiest ones to grow have hairy stems. The difficult ones are covered with scales that suggest bird droppings.

Flower description: Pink to light purple flowers are flat and wheel-shaped. They appear on and off during the year, but mostly in summer. They open in mid-afternoon, close by early evening.

Propagation: Seed or cuttings.

Culture: General succulent culture. Hairy-stemmed plants are easy to grow. Keep them lightly shaded. Although in winter they do not go completely dormant, growth slows and they need less water. Species covered with papery scales are not recommended for beginners.

Recommended species: A. lanceolata. Reddish flowers. Very long hairs on stems and leaves. Available: (15), (17), (20).

A. rufescens. Reddish purple rosettes. Pink flowers. Available: (6), (13), (16), (20), (21), (22), (24).

Ananas

Family: Bromeliaceae.

Origin: Brazil and northern South America.

General description: This is the pineapple of the grocery store. Rosettes of stiff leaves up to 3 feet long are borne on short stems. The plants spread by suckers.

Flower description: The flowers are insignificant, but the large fruit is carried on a short stem above the center of the plant. A cluster of leaves at the top of the fruit looks like a miniature plant and will grow if planted.

Propagation: Cuttings.

Culture: General succulent culture, but rich soil and plenty of water are needed to form large fruit.

Recommended species: A. comosus. This is the edible pineapple. A rosette of 3-foot-long leaves is carried on a short stem. The leaves are spiny on the edge and tip. Available: (1).

A. comosus 'Variegatus'. This cultivar is a more attractive plant for the garden than the species is. Reddish green leaves have ivory marginal stripes, and the fruit is pink. Available: (1).

Ananas comosus 'Variegatus'

Aporocactus

Family: Cactaceae.

Group: Hylocereus.

Origin: Southern Mexico, Central America.

General description: Numerous pale green, snakelike stems ½ inch in diameter, to 6 feet long. Each stem has 5 to 14 ribs. Many small bristly spines are a shade of pink when new, fading to horn-brown as they mature. Older stems develop aerial roots for gripping trees in the native habitat.

Flower description: Flowers are pink to red, funnelform, borne the length of the stem through spring, summer, and fall. They measure from 2½ to 3 inches in length and are very attractive.

Propagation: Stem cuttings, occasionally grafts of stems onto an upright rootstock.

Culture: This epiphyte is best suited to hanging-basket culture. Requires rich soil, filtered sun. Cannot tolerate frost.

Recommended species: A. flagelliformis (Rattail cactus). Crimson-pink flowers on long, slender stems. Available: (1), (13), (16), (21), (22), (27), (29), (31).

Ariocarpus

Family: Cactaceae.

Group: Echinocactus.

Origin: Mexico, Texas.

General description: Olive-brown to chalky-gray plants are round with flattened top, 6 to 10 inches in diameter. The triangular tubercles are almost leaflike. There are no spines except for a few occasional bristles at the tubercle tips.

Flower description: Pink, purple, or yellow flowers vary in size, from 1¼ inches up to 3 inches, and appear in the center of the plant in autumn. Some are urn-shaped, others wheel-shaped.

Propagation: Seed, but it takes 7 to 10 years for a plant to reach maturity.

Culture: General cactus culture. Be sure to underpot, leaving only ½ inch of room between the plant and container. Water freely from April to the end of September; taper off on watering in winter.

Recommended species: A. fissuratus. Brownish green tubercles with light magenta flowers. Available: (2), (8), (13), (15), (16), (22).

A. kotschoubeyanus. Dark olive-green tubercles. White, rose, or light purple flowers. The easiest to flower. Available: (2), (7), (9), (13), (15), (16).

A. retusus (Seven-stars). Gray or blue-green tubercles; white flowers. Available: (9), (13), (15), (16).

A. trigonus. Dark green tubercles; yellow or cream-colored flowers. The largest of the genus. Available: (9), (13), (15), (16).

Asparagus

Family: Liliaceae.

Origin: Old World, with many species in Southern Africa.

General description: Many species of *Asparagus* have tuberous roots and small, hard-surfaced leaves that reduce water loss. Growth habit is either as a woody vine or shrub. Some species have sharp spines along the stems.

Flower description: Small white flowers along the stems are followed by attractive red berries.

Propagation: Seed, division.

Culture: General succulent culture. A richer soil and generous watering will encourage growth, but the plants will survive the lack of water as well as any other succulent. These plants make excellent subjects for a hanging basket.

Recommended species: A. densiflorus 'Myers' (Foxtail asparagus). Stiff, erect stems are densely covered with short branches and bright green leaves forming a narrow tapering plume. Widely available.

A. densiflorus 'Sprengeri' (Sprenger asparagus). Similar to 'Myers' but foliage not as dense and branches more pendant. Makes an excellent hanging-basket plant. Widely available.

Astrophytum

Family: Cactaceae.

Group: Echinocactus.

Origin: Mexico.

General description: These all-green, globular to cylindrical plants have 4 to 10 ribs, and grow to between 6 inches and 2 feet in height. All except *A. ornatum* and *A. capricorne* are spineless. Several species are covered with small tufts of hair.

Flower description: All species have yellowish flowers, 1 to 4 inches across. They are funnelform or wheel-shaped and appear on the top of the plant.

Propagation: Seed. Seed-grown plants are easier to cultivate than those collected in the wild.

Culture: General cactus culture.

Aporocactus flagelliformis

Ariocarpus retusus

Astrophytum myriostigma

Aztekium ritteri

Recommended species: A. asterias (Sea urchin cactus). Dome-shaped, with 8 deeply grooved ribs. Spineless. Available: (2), (7), (8), (9), (13), (15), (22).

A. capricorne 'Aureum'. Very sharp yellow spines. Grows to 10 inches high. Available: (7), (9), (25), (31).

A. myriostigma (Bishop's-cap). White, starlike scales dot the grayish body. Most have 5 ribs. Spineless. Very old plants can reach 2 feet in height. Available: (5), (7), (8), (9), (13), (15).

A. myriostigma 'Nudum'. Dark green, ribbed body, without the dotted surface of *A. myriostigma*. Available: (7), (13), (15), (16), (22).

A. ornatum (Star cactus). Cylindrical shape to 14 inches. Yellow spines, becoming brown with age. Available: (7), (8), (13), (15), (16), (22).

Aztekium

Family: Cactaceae.
Group: Echinocactus.
Origin: Mexico.
General description: Monotypic (a genus with only one species). Globe-shaped, gray-green to green plant remains very small, forming clusters as it matures. It has alternating main and secondary ribs. The main ribs have areoles; the secondary ones do not. Very small bristles form on new areoles at the top of the plant but soon fall off.
Flower description: Miniature ½-inch funnelform flowers are white to pink. They appear on top of the plant off and on all spring and summer.
Propagation: Seed (a very slow method), or grafted offsets.
Culture: General cactus culture. Essential to keep underpotted. *Aztekium* is difficult to grow and not recommended for beginners.
Recommended species: A. ritteri. Clusters freely, forming mats, but only after attaining maximum growth. Adapts well to windowsill culture. Available: (7), (9), (16), (20), (22), (24), (25), (31).

Beaucarnea

Family: Agavaceae.
Origin: Mexico.
General description: Beaucarnea eventually grows into a tree 20 feet tall. The trunk is gray-brown and, with age, covered with bark. The swollen base gives an overall bottle appearance when young. This changes when the plant ages and begins to cluster. Long, thin, green leaves arch out all around the apex of the stem, creating a fountainlike effect.

Beaucarnea recurvata

Flower description: Insignificant flowers are beige and are borne in summer on a long stalk that rises from the top of the plant only after it is several years old.
Propagation: Seed. Plants are either male or female, so the chances of harvesting one's own seed are remote.
Culture: Given plenty of water, food, humus in the soil, and bright light, beaucarneas are fast growers. They make ideal houseplants, grow well in seemingly small pots, and need repotting only every three or four years. Due to their arching foliage, they require a fair amount of growing room.
Recommended species: B. recurvata (Elephant-foot tree, ponytail). Very long, rather sharp-edged, thin, curving green leaves. Available: (6), (7), (15), (16), (22), (25), (31).

B. stricta. Straight, glaucous green leaves have yellow margins. Available: (6), (7), (20), (22), (25).

Borzicactus

Family: Cactaceae.
Group: Cereus.
Origin: Ecuador, Chile, Bolivia, Peru.

General description: The medium to dark waxy green *Borzicactus* species can grow to a height of from 1 to 5 feet. The upright columns have distinct ribs and sharp, honey-colored spines. A few species have soft, hairy spines.

Flower description: The red tubular or funnelform flowers are usually irregularly shaped. They measure from 2 to 3 inches long and are produced near the top of the plant in summer.

Propagation: Seed and cuttings.

Culture: General cactus culture. A very robust plant, although a somewhat slow grower.

Recommended species: B. celsianus (also known as *Oreocereus celsianus*, Old-man-of-the-mountains, South American old-man). Matted hairs with yellow to red spines. Tubular red flowers. Available: (5), (7), (13), (15), (16), (20), (22).

B. trollii (also known as *Oreocereus trollii*, Old-man-of-the-Andes). Hairy with light yellow to reddish spines. Rose-colored flowers. Available: (13), (15), (16), (18), (20), (22).

Borzicactus celsianus

Bowiea

Family: Liliaceae.

Origin: South Africa, tropical East Africa.

General description: This curiosity of the plant world grows from a light green bulb that rests on the surface of the soil. Individual bulbs measure 6 inches across at maturity and occasionally form large clusters. Pale green branching stems emerge from the top of the bulb and need staking. If not supported, they will climb on anything nearby. Stems are thin and lacy, but when several grow from the same bulb they form a great spidery web.

Flower description: Greenish white flowers, 1 inch long, are produced all along the stems in great profusion from spring to fall.

Propagation: Offsets or bulb scales.

Culture: Provide ample water and well-drained soil. Feed regularly during the growing season. Stop watering and feeding when stems start to yellow and the plant goes dormant—usually in winter. *Bowiea* is an excellent houseplant, and it will thrive outdoors in the ground where there is no hard frost.

Recommended species: B. volubilis (Climbing onion). The only species currently listed in catalogs. Available: (6), (7), (31).

Bowiea volubilis

Caralluma

Family: Asclepiadaceae.

Origin: Africa to India.

General description: Clumps of leafless, finger-shaped stems range from purple-gray to green, with great variation according to species. The jointed stems, with small teeth at the angles, measure from 2 to 12 inches long, depending upon the species.

Flower description: Carallumas are grown for their brightly colored, showy flowers. They are shaped like 5-pointed stars, with colors that include cream-white, many shades of yellow, and dramatic purples and deep reds. They can be from ¼ to 4 inches across, depending on species. Flowers appear on the stems in spring, summer, and fall. While their carrion scent is strong and unpleasant, many collectors find they can overlook this drawback because of the caralluma's stunning flowers.

Propagation: Seed, cuttings.

Culture: General stapeliad culture. Carallumas range from being easy to grow to very difficult, depending on the species.

Recommended species: C. europea. Easy to grow. Yellow flowers with purple stripes and tips. Available: (7), (13), (31), (36).

C. nebrownii. Clusters of deep red-brown to blackish brown flowers. Easy to grow. Available: (5), (16), (29), (33), (36).

Caralluma nebrownii

Right: *Cephalocereus palmeri*
Far right: *Cereus peruvianus* 'Monstrosus'

Cephalocereus senilus

Cephalocereus

Family: Cactaceae.
Group: Cereus.
Origin: Mexico, South America.
General description: These upright, cylindrical cacti can reach a height of 10 feet or more, with an 8- to 10-inch diameter. The gray-green body is ribbed and has long, sharp spines. The soft hairy spines for which the genus is best known develop either before maturity or after the formation of a cephalium at the top of the plant.
Flower description: The relatively small white to red, short, funnelform flowers are borne on the top of the hairy cephalium. *Cephalocereus* does not bloom until the plant is at least 15 to 20 years old. The flowers bloom only at night.
Propagation: Seed, cuttings.
Culture: General cactus culture. Easy to care for, but slow-growing. A good windowsill specimen when young.
Recommended species: C. alensis. Long, slender stems branching from base. Brownish, needle-shaped spines on 12 to 14 ribs. Cephalium has white or yellow hairs. Purplish flowers. Available: (13), (16), (20), (24), (29).
C. palmeri (Bald old-man). Thick, bluish green, 7 to 9 ribbed stems are topped with dense, white wool, and with purplish to brownish flowers. Available: (9), (13), (15), (16), (18), (22).
C. senilis (Old-man cactus). Very popular. Woolly body with 20 to 30 ribs. Rose-colored flowers. Widely available.

Cereus

Family: Cactaceae.
Group: Cereus.
Origin: Southeastern Brazil to northern Argentina.
General description: The cylindrical, branching cereus with 4 to 8 ribs can grow to a height of 15 or 20 feet. The slender stems are blue-green to gray-green and have straight, needle-shaped radial spines.
Flower description: Large, funnelform (6- to 8-inch), white to pink flowers are produced all along the stems. They open at night during the summer.
Propagation: Seeds and cuttings.
Culture: General cactus culture. This genus is the easiest of all cacti. With generous culture, it is also the fastest growing. Size can be restricted by confining the plant to a small pot.
Recommended species: C. peruvianus (Peruvian apple). Shrubby or treelike

growth habit. Green to gray-green with 6 to 8 ribs. Available: (5), (9), (13), (15), (16), (22).

C. peruvianus 'Monstrosus' (Giant's club, curiosity plant). Approximately 12 ribs divided into irregular tubercles. Spineless. Available: (5), (9), (13), (15), (16).

Ceropegia

Family: Asclepiadaceae.

Origin: Africa.

General description: The climbing or hanging stems of ceropegias have green leaves, some with silvery markings. As a general rule, the leaves are small and quite succulent and come in widely varied and interesting shapes.

Flower description: The flowers that appear all along the vines have swollen bases and petals that are joined at the tips. The general effect is rather like a little umbrella. The majority of these unusual blossoms appear in summer, but many are also found in spring and fall.

Propagation: Cuttings, tubers, seeds.

Culture: General succulent culture, except that ceropegias need more water. They make excellent hanging-basket subjects, attractive and different houseplants.

Recommended species: *C. cimiciodora*. Very similar to *C. stapeliiformis*. Available: (7), (16), (31).

C. stapeliiformis. Thick succulent stems. White flowers 2 to 3 inches long with purple markings. Available: (31), (37).

C. woodii (Rosary vine). Dark green leaves marbled with white. Easily propagated from the tubers that form all along the stem. Flowers are about 1 inch long. Widely available.

Ceropegia woodii

Chamaecereus

Family: Cactaceae.

Group: Echinocereus.

Origin: Western Argentina.

General description: This popular monotypic species has short, clustering, green stems that grow to 6 inches long, ½ inch in diameter. They are ribbed and covered with short, bristly spines.

Flower description: *Chamaecereus* has vivid red-scarlet flowers that appear in summer all along the stems. They are a long funnelform shape, measuring approximately 3 inches.

Propagation: Cuttings.

Culture: General cactus culture. Very easy, a good beginner's plant. Does best in a shallow pot.

Recommended species: *C. sylvestri* (Peanut cactus). Widely available.

Many hybrids of *C. sylvestri* with other genera are also available. Worth watching the catalogs for.

Chamaecereus sylvestri

Cissus

Family: Vitaceae.

Origin: Southwest Africa, Tanzania, Kenya.

General description: These members of the grape family are considered most interesting by succulent collectors. They include species with enlarged, succulent trunks and others with tuberous bases that sprout vines of green leaves. In nature, the trunks can range to a maximum height of 10 feet, although those found in succulent collections are generally much smaller. The large, jagged-edged, triangular leaves and stems are deciduous.

Flower description: Small, yellowish green flowers are borne in clusters along the stems in the summer. Many species develop attractive, bright red fruit.

Cissus juttae

Cissus tuberosa

Cleistocactus hylacanthus

Cochemiea setispina

Propagation: Cuttings, seed.

Culture: General succulent culture. Winter watering must be kept to a minimum.

Recommended species: C. bainesii (also known as *Cyphostemma bainesii*, African tree grape). Yellowish green trunk. Hairy, sawtooth-edged leaves. Available: (33).

C. juttae (also known as *Cyphostemma juttae*). Fleshy bottlelike trunk with large, serrated, waxy-green leaves. Available: (31), (33).

C. quadrangula. (also known as *C. quadrangularis*, Veldt grape). Succulent vine with green, four-sided stems. Large, waxy-green leaves. Available: (20), (22), (25), (31), (33), (35).

C. tuberosa. Globe-shaped brown tuber with green, grapelike leaves. Available: (22), (25).

Cleistocactus

Family: Cactaceae.

Group: Cereus.

Origin: South America.

General description: The cylindrical green, clustering stems of *Cleistocactus* grow to a mature size of approximately 3 inches in diameter, 2 to 3 feet high. Some species grow to 10 feet high or become procumbent. The plants have many ribs and spines that vary from white to brown, dense to sparse.

Flower description: Red, scarlet, or orange flowers are borne the length of the stems during the summer. They are tubular-shaped, measuring 1½ to 4 inches long, ⅜ inch in diameter.

Propagation: Offsets, cuttings, and seeds.

Culture: General cactus culture. Good container plants. Relatively easy to grow.

Recommended species: C. baumannii (Scarlet-bugler). Erect stems to 6 feet tall with yellow to brown spines, scarlet flowers 2 to 3 inches long. Available: (9), (13), (15), (16).

C. hylacanthus. Slender erect 3-foot stems covered with many white spines. Bright red flowers. Widely available.

C. strausii (Silver-torch). Tall stems (to 6 feet) covered with white spines. Red flowers. Available: (13), (16), (20), (22), (28), (31).

Cochemiea

Family: Cactaceae.

Group: Coryphantha.

Origin: Baja California.

General description: Green cylindrical plants, some species ranging to 6 feet high. Stems cluster as the plant matures; the oldest stems occasionally become procumbent. Tubercles are arranged in a spiral. Most species have hooked central spines; some have radial spines.

Flower description: Flowers are bright red, tubular or hooded shape, measuring approximately 1 to 3 inches long, ⅜ inch in diameter. Flowers are borne on the upper axils of the plant in spring and summer.

Propagation: Seed, cuttings.

Culture: General cactus culture.

Recommended species: C. poselgeri. Trailing stems to 6 feet long. Brown spines. Available: (13), (16), (20), (28), (31).

C. setispina. To 2 feet high. Densely covered with brown-tipped white spines. Available: (13), (16), (20), (31).

Conophytum

Family: Aizoaceae.

Origin: South Africa.

General description: Like many other members of the mesembryanthe-

Far left: *Conophytum* collection
Left: *Copiapoa* species

mum mimicry group, *Conophytum* grows in stemless, clumping leaf pairs. Its round, thickly succulent foliage ranges in color from blue-green and gray-green to yellow-green. The skin is often speckled, and the leaves usually have windows at the top. The division between the leaves is a tiny slit at the top of the plant. Each year the outer shell of the old leaf pair dries and splits to expose the new leaves.

Flower description: The white to yellow dandelion-shaped flowers appear from the slit between the leaf pair, usually during winter.

Propagation: Seed, cuttings.

Culture: General mesembryanthemum culture. Due to winter blooming, summer watering must be minimal. Not recommended for beginners.

Recommended species: *C. elishae*. Bluish green leaves dotted with darker green. Bright yellow flowers. Available: (22), (24), (31), (34).

C. obcordellum (*C. nevillei*). Pale green leaves, gray-green spots. Available: (15), (22), (24), (31).

Copiapoa

Family: Cactaceae.

Group: Echinocactus.

Origin: Chile.

General description: Globe-shaped to oblong stems grow as clumps or solitary stems; all have ribs. The genus is characterized by radial spines and stems that are topped with woolly growth.

Flower description: Yellow bell-shaped to funnelform flowers appear in the spring and summer. These blooms are approximately 1½ inches long.

Propagation: Seed, cuttings.

Culture: General cactus culture.

Recommended species: *C. humilis*. Available: (5), (8), (13), (16), (31).

C. tennuisima 'Cristata'. Available: (5), (8), (13), (15), (16).

Coryphantha

Family: Cactaceae.

Group: Coryphantha.

Origin: Mexico, Cuba, southern United States.

General description: Green to gray-green stems are globular to cylindrical, solitary or clustering. All species have tubercles, some fat, others very narrow and pronounced. Spines are clustered at tubercle ends.

Flower description: The wide, funnelform flowers are usually large in relation to the plant. They appear from spring to summer and open during the day and close at night. Colors are widely varied according to species, ranging from greenish yellow to white, through pink and violet.

Propagation: Seed, cuttings.

Culture: General cactus culture.

Recommended species: *C. cornifera*. Solitary globular stems with yellowish spines, yellow flowers. Available: (13), (15), (16), (24), (28).

C. macromeris. Clustering stems with white, needle-shaped spines, purple flowers. Available: (2), (9), (15), (18), (20), (22), (24).

Coryphantha cornifera

Right: *Cotyledon undulata*
Center: *Cotyledon ladysmithiensis*
Far right: *Crassula* species

Crassula species

Crassula argentea 'Variegata'

C. macromeris var. *runyonii* (*C. runyonii*). Gray-green stems with pronounced tubercles. Purple flowers. Available: (9), (13), (15), (16).

Cotyledon

Family: Crassulaceae.

Origin: South Africa to Arabia.

General description: Cotyledons represent a large and diverse genus. They can best be characterized as shrubby succulent plants whose mature sizes range from a few inches to several feet. Most species grown by collectors have persistent, succulent leaves in colors ranging from yellow-green to blue-gray.

Flower description: Bell-shaped, yellow to red flowers are pendant on long stalks borne above the leaves during spring and summer.

Propagation: Cuttings, seed.

Culture: General succulent culture. Many cotyledons need exposure to bright light to bring out maximum foliage color.

Recommended species: *C. ladysmithiensis*. Small shrub with hairy, pale green leaves, tipped with brown. Widely available.

C. orbiculata. Red-margined leaves. Red flowers on long stalks. Available: (13), (16), (18), (20), (31), (33), (36).

C. paniculata (Botterboom). Large shrub with papery-barked trunk. Deciduous leaves. Available: (6), (16), (22), (25), (33), (36).

C. undulata (Silver-crown). Large, succulent, wavy-edged leaves. Available: (6), (13), (16), (18), (22), (24), (33).

Crassula

Family: Crassulaceae.

Origin: Southeastern Africa.

General description: This large genus of succulent shrubs can best be described as a widely diversified plant group, characterized by unusual and varied leaf forms, arrangements, and colors.

Flower description: Small white to red or yellowish flowers are borne in clusters on stems above the plants. Most crassulas bloom in spring and summer.

Propagation: Stem and leaf cuttings, seed.

Culture: General succulent culture. Crassulas are very frost-tender.

Recommended species: *C. arborescens* (Silver jade plant). Glaucous gray leaves with red margins. Plant seldom flowers. Widely available.

C. argentea (Jade tree, baby jade). Green leaves, white flowers. Requires short days (that is, winter) for flowering. Very popular. Easy to grow. Widely available.

C. falcata (Scarlet-paint-brush, airplane plant). Long, sickle-shaped, gray-green leaves. Cluster of scarlet flowers above foliage. Widely available.

C. lycopodioides (Moss crassula, rattail crassula). Slender hanging or climbing stems with tiny, green, scalelike leaves. Widely available.

C. 'Morgan's Pink'. Fragrant salmon to rose-colored flowers, small clustering leaves. Widely available.

C. *perforata* (String-of-buttons). Widely available.

C. *teres* (Rattlesnake). Narrow, cylindrical plant composed of closely overlapping pale green leaves. Widely available.

Cryptanthus

Family: Bromeliaceae.

Origin: Brazil.

General description: These low-growing terrestrial bromeliads form rosettes from 6 inches to 2 feet in diameter. Most carry their leaves flattened against the ground, hence the common name, earth star. The stiff leaves may be green or brown and are often banded with white. Older plants form clumps.

Flower description: Flowers are small, greenish or white, and are borne on very short stems in the center of the plant.

Propagation: Seed, cuttings.

Culture: General succulent culture. They need shade for best growth and color but will tolerate brighter light.

Recommended species: C. *acaulis* (Starfish plant). The stemless leaves have wavy edges and form rosettes up to 1 foot in diameter. Leaf color varies from green to brown, and many cultivars are available with different banding patterns on the leaf. Widely available.

C. *beuckeri*. Green leaves banded with white are carried on a short stem. Plants are 6 to 12 inches tall. Available: (1), (12), (17), (35).

C. 'It'. An unusual cultivar with red and white stripes running the length of 10-inch leaves. Available: (1), (12), (17), (35).

Cryptanthus species

Cycas revoluta

Cycas

Family: Cycadaceae.

Origin: Old World tropics.

General description: These palmlike plants have thick, succulent trunks that bear a crown of leaves with many stiff, narrow, green leaflets. Members of the closely related genera—*Ceratozamia, Dioon, Enchephalartos*, and *Zamia*—share cycas' leaf arrangement, although leaf color, texture, and shape are varied. All are very slow growing, but a well-established plant will live for many years.

Flower description: Cycas bears large, loose cones at the top of the trunk when mature. Female plants have larger cones. Plants are either male or female, and both sexes must bear cones simultaneously to produce viable seed.

Propagation: Offsets, seed.

Culture: These easy but slow-growing plants are good landscape subjects in frost-free climates. They make ideal houseplants and attractive "bonsai" specimens.

Recommended species: C. *revoluta* (Sago palm). A popular "bonsai" specimen. Available: (15), (25), (31), (32).

Dasylirion

Family: Agavaceae.

Origin: Southwestern United States, Mexico.

General description: The very long, slender, stemless leaves of dasylirion form a fountainlike rosette up to 6 feet in diameter. The leaves usually have small teeth on their margins.

Flower description: Cream-white flowers are borne in clusters on a long stalk in spring and summer.

Propagation: Seed.

Culture: General succulent culture.

Dasylirion wheeleri

Dinteranthus puberulus

Dioscorea elephantipes

Recommended species: *D. wheeleri*. Old plants will develop a short trunk. Yellow, tooth-edged, green leaves. Widely available.

Dinteranthus

Family: Aizoaceae.

Origin: South Africa.

General description: Thickly succulent leaf pairs are pale and stemless and mimic surrounding stones in their native habitat. These small leaf pairs grow in clumps that rarely exceed 6 inches in diameter.

Flower description: Yellow dandelionlike flowers appear in winter at the split between the leaf pair.

Propagation: Seed.

Culture: General mesembryanthemum culture. Growth during the summer requires careful watering. Keep absolutely dry during the winter. Not recommended for beginners.

Recommended species: *D. puberulus* (Flowering-stone). Brownish gray-green skin with dark green dots. Available: (2), (5), (22), (36).

Dioscorea

Family: Dioscoreaceae.

Origin: Mexico, South Africa.

General description: The distinctive brown caudex of *Dioscorea* resembles a tortoise shell. It can range in size from 4 inches to 2 feet in diameter. A thin vine, which can be up to 30 feet long, emerges from the tuber. It has small, green, heart-shaped leaves. During the dioscorea's 3- to 4-month-long dormancy, both leaves and vine are usually dropped.

Flower description: Clusters of small, starlike, greenish yellow flowers appear in late summer. They are insignificant. *Dioscorea* is cultivated more for its unusual caudex than as a foliage or flower plant.

Propagation: Seed.

Culture: The cultural needs of *Dioscorea* are closer to those of common houseplants than of succulents. The plant should be placed in a container with about an inch of very porous soil above the outer edge of the tuber. *Dioscorea* should not be allowed to dry out completely between waterings.

Recommended species: *D. elephantipes* (Elephant's foot). Caudex resembles a tortoise shell. Twining stems. Native to South Africa. Available: (6), (9), (20), (25).

D. macrostachya. Native to Mexico. Available: (6), (9), (20), (31).

Diplocyatha ciliata

Diplocyatha

Family: Asclepiadaceae.

Origin: South Africa.

General description: The gray-green, leafless succulent stems of *Diplocyatha* grow in small clusters, seldom exceeding 3 inches long. They have riblike angles that are armed with soft teeth.

Flower description: Like other stapeliads, *Diplocyatha* has dramatic, starfish-shaped flowers. The beige 3-inch diameter flowers are spotted with maroon, and appear from the base of the stems during the growing season. Flowers are rimmed with hanging tassels.

Propagation: Cuttings.

Culture: General stapeliad culture. *Diplocyatha* is among the most easily cultivated stapeliads.

Recommended species: *D. ciliata* (*Orbea ciliata*). Available: (5), (7), (15).

Dolichothele

Family: Cactaceae.

Group: Coryphantha.

Origin: Mexico.

General description: The clustering, globe-shaped stems have green tubercles. Depending upon the species, each head can measure up to 5 inches in diameter. Clusters of spines are found at the tubercles' tips.

Flower description: Yellow, funnelform flowers, generally large in relation to the plant, are borne in the upper tubercle axils in spring and summer.

Propagation: Seed, cuttings.

Culture: General cactus culture.

Recommended species: *D. sphaerica* (*Mammillaria longimamma*). Fat green tubercles with radial spines. Available: (2), (9), (15), (18), (20), (22), (24).

Dolichothele species

Dudleya

Family: Crassulaceae.

Origin: Washington State to Baja California.

General description: The succulent, long-triangular or spindle-shaped leaves of *Dudleya* species form rosettes borne on fleshy stems that can grow quite long. The largest species of the genus grows to a maximum diameter of 1½ feet. Smaller-growing species seldom surpass 6 to 8 inches. The most distinctive characteristic of *Dudleya* species is the light green foliage. Once the plant has matured, a powdery white bloom appears on the leaves of some species, giving them a luminous glow. The foliage should not be touched after the bloom has appeared.

Flower description: Small, star-shaped, orange, yellow, or white flowers are borne in clusters on an upright stalk. Flowering generally occurs in early spring to early summer.

Propagation: Cuttings, seed.

Culture: General succulent culture, except that plants tend to want more water in winter and spring than in summer and fall.

Recommended species: *D. brittonii*. Solitary rosettes of powdery white leaves to 1½ feet across. Available: (6), (13), (16), (22), (31).

D. farinosa. Small rosettes. Pale yellow flowers. Available: (13), (16), (22), (33).

Dudleya brittonii

Dyckia

Family: Bromeliaceae.

Origin: Brazil, Paraguay, Argentina.

General description: Stemless rosettes of green- to maroon-colored leaves often form large clumps. The foliage is stiff, armed with sharply pointed tips and spiny margins. A silvery overlay on the leaves of some species gives these plants an attractive appearance.

Flower description: Yellow, orange, or red flowers are borne on tall, slender stalks. There are many small blooms in each cluster. Dyckias bloom in the spring.

Propagation: Seed, division.

Culture: *Dyckia* species are well suited to being grown as rock-garden specimens in frost-free climates. They also make excellent container-grown greenhouse specimens.

Dyckia fosterana

Recommended species: *D. fosterana*. A 4-inch rosette of silvery leaves, which become bronzed when grown in full sun. Spiny leaf margins. Bright gold flowers. Available: (32), (33).

D. marnier-lapostollei. A recent discovery. Thick, short leaves have soft, velvety hairs and spiny margins. Available: (32), (33).

D. remotiflora. Silvery green leaves taper to a needlelike point. Large orange-red flowers. Available: (32), (33).

Echeveria

Family: Crassulaceae.

Origin: Mexico to Venezuela.

General description: All echeverias grow in a rosette form, but their leaf

Echeveria pulvinata

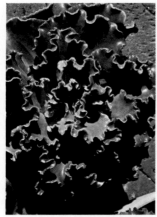

Echeveria hybrid

Echinocactus grusonii

Echinocactus grusonii

colors vary greatly, ranging from pale green through deep purple. Many are luminous pink. In general, the hairy-leaved species and hybrids are smaller growers, with narrow, less succulent leaves. Many smooth-skinned species have very wide, thickly succulent leaves that form a large rosette (to 16 inches) resembling a head of leaf lettuce. Most echeverias are stemless or have very short stems.

Flower description: The long-lasting pendant flowers are red, pink, or orange, borne on a stalk above the rosette. Each flower ranges in size from ¼ to 1 inch long, ¼ to ⅜ inch in diameter. Blooming occurs in spring, summer, or fall, depending upon the species.

Propagation: Cuttings of leaves, flower stalks, or offsets at base; occasionally from seed.

Culture: General succulent culture. *Echeveria* species usually do well under generous cultural practices—more water, more fertilizer, and a richer soil than is required by many succulents. Exposure to light increases the intensity of leaf color. If the stems become leggy, the growing tip can be cut off and rerooted.

Recommended species: E. affinis. Bright green to greenish black oblong leaves; red flowers. Widely available.

E. agavoides (Molded wax). Shiny green leaves tinged with dark red. Red flowers tipped with yellow. Widely available.

E. 'Black Prince'. A hybrid with deep maroon foliage. Available: (5), (15), (22), (31), (35), (36).

E. derenbergii (Painted-lady). Many thickly succulent, small, pointed, glaucous blue leaves form a tight rosette. Widely available.

E. elegans (Pearl echeveria, Mexican-gem). Tight rosette of small, glaucous green leaves. Rose flowers tipped with yellow. Widely available.

E. 'Morning Light'. A hybrid with beautiful luminous pink foliage. Available: (18), (22), (35).

E. pulvinata (Plush plant, chenille plant). Narrow, dark green leaves covered with many fine, short hairs. Edges of foliage tinged with red. Widely available.

In addition to the species and hybrids listed above, there are many other fascinating and beautiful members of this large genus, all worthwhile choices for any collector.

Echinocactus

Family: Cactaceae.
Group: Echinocactus.
Origin: Texas to Mexico.
General description: Shiny, green, globe-shaped echinocacti are popular for their form and numerous sharp, brightly colored spines, which range from straw yellow to shades of red. In time they can grow to a very large size—up to 3 feet or more in diameter. When young, they have tubercles, which turn into ribs as the plants mature.

Flower description: These 2-inch-long, pink to yellow, bell-shaped flowers are borne on the top, woolly parts of the plant in summer.

Propagation: Seed.

Culture: General cactus culture. Relatively easy to grow, *Echinocactus* species make good houseplants, tolerating low light indoors.

Recommended species: E. grusonii (Golden barrel cactus). Widely available.

Echinocereus

Family: Cactaceae.
Group: Echinocereus.
Origin: Southwest United States and Mexico.
General description: Members of the genus *Echinocereus* are generally upright, cylindrical plants, measuring from 2 to 4 inches thick, and up to

Far left: *Echinocereus* species
Left: *Echinopsis* hybrid

2 feet high. They have numerous ribs; spinal arrangement and color are widely varied among the species.

Flower description: Flowers, ranging from funnelform to bell-shaped, are predominantly metallic purple, but a few species have yellow or pink blooms. The blossoms, usually measuring from 1 to 5 inches, appear near the top of the plant in late spring or summer.

Propagation: Seed and cuttings.

Culture: General cactus culture. Species native to Mexico are generally easier to grow than those native to the United States.

Recommended species: E. cinerascens. White, needle-shaped spines. Rose to purple flowers. Available: (13), (15), (16), (18), (20), (28).

E. enneacanthus var. *conglomeratus* (*E. conglomeratus*, strawberry cactus). Many clustering stems densely covered with straw-colored spines. Purplish red flowers. Not recommended for beginners. Available: (13), (16), (20), (28).

E. knippelianus. Solitary, dark green stems, yellow spines, pink flowers. Not recommended for beginners. Widely available.

Echinopsis

Family: Cactaceae.

Group: Echinocereus.

Origin: South America.

General description: Echinopsis species are characterized by gray-green to green globular to oval stems that grow singly or in clusters. They are distinctly ribbed, occasionally with a few tubercles, and clusters of spines on areoles along the ribs.

Flower description: This genus is best known for its long-lasting, large, funnelform flowers. They range from white to pink, and are frequently up to 8 inches long.

Propagation: Seed.

Culture: General cactus culture. Small-growing, free-flowering species make good windowsill specimens.

Recommended species: E. 'Haku-jo'. A recently discovered sport, grown for its dark green body. Available: (5), (20), (22), (24), (31).

Because *Echinopsis* has been extensively crossbred with *Lobivia* and *Trichocereus*, many nurseries list "*E. hyb.*" and give a description of flower color. These hybrids are worth trying.

Edithcolea

Family: Asclepiadaceae.

Origin: Socotra Island and Somalia.

General description: Edithcolea has succulent beige and brown stems that sprawl and creep. They are angled and covered with small teeth. The plants are leafless.

Flower description: Edithcolea is grown for its beautiful flowers. They are very large (up to 4 inches), star-shaped, yellow with dark maroon markings. These flowers appear in summer.

Echinopsis species

Edithcolea grandis

Epiphyllum hybrid

Epiphyllum hybrid

Epithelantha micromeris

Propagation: Cuttings, seed.

Culture: Very difficult to grow and recommended only for the most advanced collector. Soil must be very porous, preferably high in pumice. Water frequently during the summer, not at all in winter.

Recommended species: E. grandis. Available: (9), (16), (31), (33).

Epiphyllum

Family: Cactaceae.

Group: Hylocereus.

Origin: American tropics.

General description: These tropical epiphytes have long green stems that hang or climb. The oldest stems are often cylindrical, becoming woody with age. Younger branches are flat or have 3 ribs. Some species are spineless; others have tiny, bristly spines clustered at intervals along the stem margins.

Flower description: Epiphyllums are grown for their large, showy blooms. Most species have white flowers; the extensively hybridized cultivars range through red, yellow, orange, and pink, many having intense coloration. The flowers are borne along the length of the stems, opening during the day or at night (depending upon the species), in the spring and early summer.

Propagation: Cuttings, seed.

Culture: General tropical cactus culture. Epiphyllums need a soil rich in humus, and filtered sun. They are perfectly suited to hanging-basket culture.

Recommended species: E. chrysocardium. Available: (35).

Many beautiful hybrids (shown in the photos here) are available from specialist nurseries. Write for catalogs: (11), (14), (30).

Epithelantha

Family: Cactaceae.

Group: Echinocactus.

Origin: Texas to Mexico.

General description: The globular to short, cylindrical clustering stems of *Epithelantha* are usually white. They grow to a maximum height of 4 inches. They have tubercles and many small white spines.

Flower description: Small white to pink flowers are borne on the top of the plant from spring through fall. The fruit formed by pollinated flowers is interesting—it sits up like tiny pink fingers around the top of the plant.

Propagation: Seed, offsets.

Culture: General cactus culture. *Epithelantha* is somewhat fussy about light requirements. It likes a sunny spot but cannot tolerate full sun all day.

Recommended species: E. micromeris (Button cactus). Globular stems with depressed apex. Widely available.

Escobaria

Family: Cactaceae.

Group: Coryphantha.

Origin: Texas to Mexico.

General description: Escobaria, often considered a subgenus of *Coryphantha*, is characterized by whitish cylindrical stems that grow to a maximum height of 8 inches. The stems have fat to triangular tubercles and numerous short white spines with dark tips.

Flower description: White to pink small funnelform flowers appear at the top of the plant in spring and summer.

Propagation: Seed, offsets.

Culture: General cactus culture. These plants need a very open soil mix and careful watering.

Recommended species: E. dasyacantha. Dark-tipped, bristlelike spines. Pink flowers. Available: (13), (16), (28), (31).

Espostoa

Family: Cactaceae.
Group: Cereus.
Origin: Peru, Brazil.
General description: The columnar stems of *Espostoa* have many ribs. In general, the branching stems are very tall and slender, reaching to 18 feet in height. Soft, hairy, white and stouter yellowish spines are along the ribs.
Flower description: Nocturnal white flowers are borne on a lateral cephalium, composed of specialized, hairy areoles on one side of the stem. Blossoms are funnelform, to 2 inches long.
Propagation: Seed.
Culture: General cactus culture.
Recommended species: E. lanata (Cotton-ball, Peruvian old-man). Grows to 18 feet. White wool with yellow or brownish spines. Widely available.
E. melanostele. Brown wool; long, black spines. Widely available.

Euphorbia

Family: Euphorbiaceae.
Origin: Worldwide, but most of the succulent species are from Africa.
General description: The genus *Euphorbia* is too diverse to allow more than a few generalizations. All species have a milky sap of varying toxicity; many are succulent. Mature sizes can range from a few inches to many feet. The succulent *Euphorbia* species have leaves that are generally insignificant and deciduous. Many species have spines, although unlike those of cacti they do not grow out of areoles. In some instances the spines are actually dried flower stalks.
Flower description: Euphorbia flowers are usually quite small, often yellow or greenish yellow. The flower consists only of a unisexual male stamen or female pistil, generally clustered together and sometimes surrounded by colorful bracts (specialized leaves). Time of bloom for euphorbias depends upon both species and cultural conditions.
Propagation: Easiest from cuttings. Sap must be coagulated by immersion in cold water or powdered charcoal. Allow callus to form, then place in soil. Grafting is possible, provided another euphorbia (*E. mammillaris* or *E. cereiformis*) is used as a rootstock. Cuts must be coagulated and cleaned before grafting. Seed, when obtainable, is another acceptable method.
Culture: General succulent culture. As a rule, euphorbias require a slightly richer soil than do most cacti. They make good houseplants, unbothered by low humidity. Euphorbias need bright light; they grow well under artificial lights.
Recommended species: E. flanaganii 'Cristata'. Ribbed, spiny, green stems. Widely available.
E. grandicornis (Cow's-horn). Succulent, spiny, branching gray-green stems. Widely available.
E. horrida (African milk barrel). Many spiny, succulent ribs. Widely available.
E. mammillaris hybrid (Corkscrew). Dwarf, clustering, tubercled cylinders. Widely available.
E. milii (E. spendens, crown-of-thorns). Thin-stemmed, spiny shrub with green leaves, bright pink bracts. Widely available.
E. obesa (Living-baseball). Spineless, globe-shaped succulent with gray and green markings. Individual male and female plants. Very unusual. Widely available.
E. pseudocactus. Spiny, columnar, ribbed succulent. Widely available.
E. splendens. (See: E. milii.)
E. submammillaris 'Corn Cob'. As the name implies, it looks like a corn cob. Widely available.

Espostoa species

Euphorbia milii

Euphorbia pseudocactus and *E. obesa*

Faucaria

Family: Aizoaceae.

Origin: South Africa.

General description: Very short-stemmed, succulent, triangular-shaped leaves have small teeth along their margins. The leaves grow in small, low clumps, ranging in color from glaucous green to olive green, often with spotting on the skin.

Flower description: Typical of the mesembryanthemums, *Faucaria* has dandelionlike, yellow to white flowers that open in summer.

Propagation: Seed.

Culture: General mesembryanthemum culture. A good plant for beginners.

Recommended species: F. *tigrina* (Tiger's-jaws). Gray-green skin with white dots. Yellow flowers. Widely available.

F. *tuberculosa.* Dark green leaves with white warts on upperside. Available: (7), (9), (15), (22).

Faucaria tigrina

Fenestraria

Family: Aizoaceae.

Origin: South Africa.

General description: The thickly succulent, dull green, stemless leaves of *Fenestraria* clump to form a 2- to 2½-inch rosette. They have windows at the tops of their stems. In nature, the whole plant lies buried in gravelly soil with only the windows exposed at the soil surface.

Flower description: Daisy-shaped yellow or white flowers are borne on a short stem above the leaves. Blossoms are relatively large, measuring from 2 to 3 inches in diameter. Plants flower in summer.

Propagation: Seed.

Culture: General mesembryanthemum culture. Not recommended for beginners. Watering and light requirements are quite precise.

Recommended species: F. *aurantiaca.* Orange-yellow flowers. Widely available.

F. *rhopalophylla* (Window plant, baby-toes). Glaucous green leaves with white flowers. Available: (13), (15), (16).

Fenestraria rhopalophylla

Ferocactus

Family: Cactaceae.

Group: Echinocactus.

Origin: Southwestern United States, Mexico.

General description: The globe-shaped to columnar *Ferocactus* species vary in color from blue-green to green, with approximately 10 to 20 ribs. Their highly interesting, widely varied spines range from yellow to red. Most of them are very sharp and strong. Some species develop wool upon flowering.

Flower description: The yellow to red-purple flowers are funnelform to tulip-shaped, measuring 2 to 3 inches in length. They appear at the top of mature plants in summer.

Propagation: Seed.

Culture: General cactus culture. A good container plant. Slow growing.

Recommended species: F. *echidne.* Globe-shaped cactus with straight yellow spines, yellow flowers. Available: (2), (13), (16), (20), (24), (28).

F. *glaucescens* (Blue-barrel cactus). A very distinct glaucous green with pale yellow spines, yellow flowers. Available: (13), (15), (16), (20), (24), (28).

F. *latispinus* (Devil's-tongue). Depressed globe-shaped plant with yellow radial spines, heavy red central spines. Purple-colored flowers. Available: (2), (5), (9), (13), (15), (16), (22).

F. *macrodiscus.* Depressed globe shape with curved spines, pink flowers. Available: (13), (15), (16), (28), (31).

Ferocactus macrodiscus

F. wislizenii (Fishhook cactus). Columnar with 2-inch white radial spines; red, brown, or gray hooked central spines to 4 inches long. Orange-red to yellow flowers. Available: (2), (13), (15), (16).

Fouquieria

Family: Fouquieriaceae.

Origin: Southwestern United States, Mexico.

General description: These treelike shrubs have spiny trunks with short lateral branches which intermittently bear green leaves. Height varies according to the species.

Flower description: The genus has two basic flower types: one small, bell-shaped and creamy white; the other long (1 to 1½ inches), tubular, and reddish. They are borne in clusters on the stems. Flowering time is after the spring rains.

Propagation: Cuttings, seed.

Culture: General succulent culture. *Fouquieria* requires a slightly more generous ration of water than do many succulents.

Recommended species: F. columnaris (*Idria columnaris*, boojum tree). Conical trunk with short spreading branches and white flowers. Mature height to 50 feet. Small plants make good "bonsai" subjects. Available: (7), (25), (33).

F. splendens (Ocotillo, coach-whip). Shrub to 20 feet high with tubular red flowers. Available: (1), (7), (18), (20), (25).

Fouquieria splendens

Frailea

Family: Cactaceae.

Group: Echinocactus.

Origin: South America.

General description: Small-growing cacti that are generally wider than they are high, *Frailea* species grow in clusters reaching a maximum of 2 feet. Stems are ribbed; skin is usually a shade of green, sometimes with purple markings. Spines range from numerous and bristlelike to sparse and much stouter.

Flower description: One rarely sees the yellow flowers of frailea. They open only under the hottest, brightest sun. When open, they are funnelform, approximately 1½ inches long. Flowers that remain closed are self-pollinating; those that open must be pollinated by hand.

Propagation: Seed, cuttings.

Culture: General cactus culture.

Recommended species: F. cataphracta. Crescent-shaped purple markings below areoles. Bristlelike yellowish spines. Available: (13), (16), (20), (28), (31).

F. grahliana. Top-shaped stems with curved yellow spines. Available: (13), (16), (20), (22), (24), (29), (31).

F. schilinzkyana. Depressed globular stems with black spines. Available: (15), (16), (20), (21).

Frailea species

Gasteria

Family: Liliaceae.

Origin: South Africa.

General description: The stemless leaves of *Gasteria* species form rosettes as the plants mature. The foliage is succulent, generally green to dark green with darker spotted markings. Some species have cream-colored markings with pink-tinged margins. Leaves measure to 1½ inches wide, 18 inches long, although they are much smaller in many species.

Flower description: Curving tubular flowers measure 1 to 2 inches long. The red-orange blooms are borne on a long, nodding stalk during the summer.

Gasteria hybrid

Graptopetalum paraguayense

Propagation: Offsets, seed.

Culture: General succulent culture. Gasterias can be grown in relatively shady locations.

Recommended species: G. armstrongii. White markings on spiral leaf rosettes in older plants. Available: (13), (16), (18), (21), (22), (25).

G. caespitosa (Pencil-leaf). Narrow leaves spotted with light green. Available: (13), (16), (18), (21), (22), (25).

Graptopetalum

Family: Crassulaceae.

Origin: Southwestern United States, Mexico.

General description: Attractive rosettes of thickly succulent leaves are borne on long stems. The leaves are a luminous white with pink-purple tones. Mature rosettes measure approximately 3 inches in diameter.

Flower description: Straw-colored flowers with maroon markings are bell-shaped, usually carried on a pendant stalk in the summer.

Propagation: Stem or leaf cuttings.

Culture: General succulent culture. *Graptopetalum* is very easy to grow. It is particularly well-suited to being grown in a hanging basket.

Recommended species: G. paraguayense (Ghost plant, mother-of-pearl plant). A good beginner's plant. Available in many retail garden centers and plant shops. Catalogs: (7), (15), (20), (22), (24), (33), (35).

Gymnocalycium

Family: Cactaceae.

Group: Echinocactus.

Origin: Argentina to Brazil.

General description: The globular stems of *Gymnocalycium* species grow in clusters or singly, each stem measuring to 12 inches thick, depending upon species. The green to gray-green cacti have tubercled ribs and clusters of stout, but relatively sparse spines.

Flower description: The white to pink flowers are borne near the top of the plant in spring and summer. The edges of their petals are often green or purple. They are bell-shaped to short funnelform, measuring up to 3 inches long.

Propagation: Seed.

Culture: General cactus culture.

Recommended species: G. baldianum. Dark gray-green stems; wine-red flowers. Available: (13), (15), (16), (18), (20), (24), (31).

G. denudatum (Spider cactus). Yellowish, needle-shaped spines. White to pale rose flowers. Widely available.

G. saglione. Solitary stems to 12 inches thick. White or pink flowers. Available: (5), (8), (13), (15), (16).

Gymnocalycium species

Right: *Gymnocalycium saglione*
Far right: *Gymnocalycium denudatum*

Hamatocactus

See: Ferocactus.

Hatiora

Family: Cactaceae.
Group: Rhipsalis.
Origin: Brazil.
General description: The leafless, jointed stems of *Hatiora* form small pendant bushes growing to a maximum of 18 inches in diameter. The stems are spineless.
Flower description: A profusion of round, bright yellow flowers with red markings are borne in the axils of the stems during the spring and summer.
Propagation: Cuttings, sometimes seed.
Culture: General tropical cactus culture. This epiphyte requires a humus-rich soil, filtered sun.
Recommended species: H. *salicornioides* (Spice cactus, drunkard's dream). Available: (20), (22), (24), (28), (29), (31).

Hatiora salicornioides

Haworthia

Family: Liliaceae.
Origin: South Africa.
General description: Stemless leaves form rosettes ranging from 1 to 6 inches in diameter. Many leaves are shaped like long, narrow triangles. They are primarily dark green with many color variations, including blue-green, red, and brown. They are accented with white markings that are tiny warts. Species with shorter, more succulent, smooth-skinned leaves are more sun tolerant. They are generally a lighter green and have windows along their upper surfaces for filtering sunlight.
Flower description: The small, relatively insignificant flowers are borne in clusters on long stems from the center of the plant. Flowers are usually white with stripes of light green or pale pink. Flowering can be at any time of year, depending on the species.
Propagation: Division. Occasionally, cuttings are made of slow-growing species. Seed possible but unreliable.
Culture: General succulent culture. Haworthias can tolerate shady conditions, but need bright light (not full sun) to bring out maximum coloration and texture. Requirements vary with each species. Dormancy can occur in summer or winter, depending upon species, and can be accompanied by root loss. Plants with dead or dying roots should be cleaned and repotted in fresh soil. Narrow-leaved haworthias require more water than do many succulents. Thickly succulent species and plants with large tap roots must be watered carefully year-round.
Recommended species: H. *attenuata*. Long, dark green leaves with white markings. Shade lover. Available: (13), (15), (16), (22), (31), (33).

H. *cuspidata*. Pale green, thickly succulent leaves with windows. Widely available.

H. *fasciata* (Zebra haworthia). Glossy green, long, triangular leaves with white markings. Widely available.

H. *limifolia* (Fairy-washboard). Dark green-brown, ribbed leaves. Widely available.

H. *margaritifera* (Pearl plant). Dark green leaves with white tubercles. Widely available.

H. *retusa*. Pale green, thickly succulent leaves with windows, pointed tips. Widely available.

H. *tessellata*. Succulent, dark green, triangular leaves with windows, pale green markings. Widely available.

H. *truncata*. Dark greenish brown, thickly succulent leaves with windows. Widely available.

Haworthia collection

Haworthia species

Haworthia truncata

Hechtia

Family: Bromeliaceae.

Origin: Mexico and Central America.

General description: The tough, succulent leaves are spiny and toothed and grow in low rosettes after forming large and impenetrable clumps. Rosettes grow to 3 feet in diameter on 3-foot stems in the larger species. Leaf color is green to red, often with a powdery surface texture.

Flower description: Small white to orange or rose-colored flowers are carried on a straight 3- to 6-foot flower stalk.

Propagation: Seed, division.

Culture: General succulent culture. The best leaf color is developed in full sun. Good rock garden plants but best kept away from areas with heavy traffic because of nasty spines on the leaves.

Recommended species: H. glomerata. Glossy, spiny leaves grow to 1½ feet long on stemless plants in clumps. The leaves develop red and brown coloring in bright light. Flowers are borne on 2 to 3 spikes, 2 feet tall, from each rosette. Available: (1).

H. marnier-lapostollei. A dwarf species with silver-gray fleshy leaves. The leaf surface has a silvery appearance due to a coating of fine powderlike scale. Available: (1).

Homalocephala

See: Echinocactus.

Hoya

Family: Asclepiadaceae.

Origin: China, India, Malayan archipelago, Australia.

General description: Hoyas grow as evergreen climbing or twining vines, or as loose shrubs. The succulent species have green, waxy-looking leaves.

Flower description: Fragrant clusters of star-shaped flowers are borne on short spurs along the stems in summer and fall. Colors are generally yellow to white, with red, purple, or brown markings. Flower spurs should never be cut off because they are the growing point for the next crop of flowers.

Propagation: Cuttings.

Culture: General stapeliad culture. Hoyas prefer well-drained, moderately rich soil and filtered sun.

Recommended species: H. bella (Miniature wax plant). Many-branched dwarf shrub. Flowers are white with deep crimson centers. An excellent hanging-basket plant. Available: (20), (25), (29), (31).

H. carnosa (Wax plant). Succulent shrub with trailing stems; flowers are white with red centers. Many cultivars are available with variation in leaf texture and color: (7), (18), (20), (22), (29), (33), (37).

Huernia

Family: Asclepiadaceae.

Origin: South Africa, East Africa, Arabia.

General description: The soft, fleshy, gray-green species of *Huernia* grow in large clumps and have prominent but soft teeth. Measuring approximately ½ inch across and 2 to 3 inches in length, they look somewhat like jointed fingers.

Flower description: Huernias are cultivated for their yellow, red-brown, or dark maroon flowers. These star- to urn-shaped blooms measure from ⅜ to 3 inches across, generally appearing from the base of the stems in summer and early fall. They have mild but not offensive carrion scent.

Propagation: Cuttings, seed.

Culture: General stapeliad culture.

Recommended species: H. hystrix. Crimson markings on yellow flowers. Available: (7), (9), (16), (33), (36).

Hoya bella

Huernia pillansii

H. pillansii (Cocklebur). Stems densely covered with bristly teeth. Flowers are pale yellow spotted with crimson. Available: (5), (13), (15), (16), (22), (24).

H. schneiderana (Red dragon flower). Hairy, brownish red flowers with purple-black tubes. Available: (7), (13), (16), (22), (33).

Hylocereus

Family: Cactaceae.

Group: Hylocereane.

Origin: American tropics.

General description: The slender, 3-ribbed, light green to yellow-green stems of the hylocereus climb or hang. In their native habitat they sometimes reach great lengths. They have short, sparse spines.

Flower description: Hylocereus is grown mainly for its fragrant, very large white flowers. (Some species are red.) The funnelform blooms are to 12 inches long, 15 inches wide. Nocturnal bloomers, they open all along the stems in spring and summer.

Propagation: Cuttings, seed.

Culture: General tropical cactus culture. Cannot stand heavy frost. Best suited to hanging-basket culture.

Recommended species: H. undatus (Night-blooming cereus, queen-of-the-night). Beautiful white flowers. Available: (9), (18), (20), (21), (22), (31).

Hylocereus undatus

Jatropha

Family: Euphorbiaceae.

Origin: Tropical regions of the world.

General description: The caudex (swollen stem) of the jatropha is gray. It has shrubby green foliage that drops off during winter dormancy.

Flower description: Small, star-shaped, red flowers are borne in clusters on annual stems in the summer.

Propagation: Seed.

Culture: General succulent culture. Do not water during dormancy.

Recommended species: J. berlandieri. (See: *J. cathartica.*)

J. cathartica (*J. berlandieri*). Slow-growing, with spherical caudex. Available: (5), (7), (13), (15), (16), (22), (32), (37).

J. podagrica (Bottle plant). Swollen trunk to 1½ feet tall with round, hand-shaped leaves. Available: (31), (37).

Jatropha cathartica

Kalanchoe

Family: Crassulaceae.

Origin: Tropical regions of the world, primarily Africa and Madagascar.

General description: Plants in this large genus are generally shrubby, ranging in size from a few inches to several feet. They are best known for their attractive, colorful leaves. They can be found in all shades of green, gray-green, blue-green, even bronzy browns and reds. Some leaves are variegated, some hairy, some smooth.

Flower description: The red, yellow, or white bell-shaped flowers of the kalanchoe are usually borne on stalks near the top of the plant during spring, summer, and fall.

Propagation: Seed, cuttings, and cuttings of plantlets formed in leaf notches.

Culture: General succulent culture. Relatively easy to grow. These plants will *not* tolerate frost.

Recommended species: K. beharensis (Feltbush, velvetleaf). Large, triangular, scalloped leaves, covered with tiny hairs. Leaves are clustered at the tips of branches. Available: (13), (16), (20), (21), (24), (36).

K. blossfeldiana. Long-lasting blooms of scarlet, yellow, and orange are borne in clusters above green foliage in winter. Extensively hybridized. Widely available in retail nurseries and plant stores.

Kalanchoe beharensis

Lapidaria margaretae

Lemaireocereus species

Leuchtenbergia principis

K. *pumila*. Small, scallop-edged leaves. Rose to violet flowers. Widely available.

K. *tomentosa* (Pussy-ears, panda plant). Gray-green leaves are covered with silvery hairs, tipped with brown. Very popular. Widely available.

Lapidaria

Family: Aizoaceae.

Origin: Southwest Africa.

General description: This monotypic species is another example of mesembryanthemum mimicry plants. The smooth-skinned, stemless pairs of leaves resemble very pale green stones. The thickly succulent leaves are approximately 1 inch long, ⅜ inch in diameter.

Flower description: Daisylike flowers are yellow to cream-white, fading to pink as they age. The 1½- to 2-inch flowers appear in the summer.

Propagation: Seed, sometimes offsets.

Culture: General mesembryanthemum culture. Not recommended for beginners.

Recommended species: L. *margaretae* (Karoo rose). The only species of genus *Lapidaria*. Available: (5), (15), (16), (22), (24), (31), (34).

Lemaireocereus

Family: Cactaceae.

Group: Cereus.

Origin: North and South America.

General description: The 3 to 20 ribbed, columnar *Lemaireocereus* species can grow to a height of 10 to 20 feet or more. They have a dull green skin and sharp spines that vary from 1 inch to 6 inches in length.

Flower description: *Lemaireocereus* bloom only when they are very old. Flowers vary from straw-colored to pale pink. They are borne along the sides on the ribs.

Propagation: Seed, offsets.

Culture: General cactus culture. *Very* easy to grow. Though they will eventually outgrow a container, they can remain potted specimens for a long time.

Recommended species: L. *marginatus* (Organ-pipe cactus). Branching green cactus with needle-shaped spines. Available: (5), (9), (15), (20), (22), (26), (28).

L. *pruinosis* (Powder-blue cereus). Thick, glaucous green stems, white to rose flowers. Available: (5), (14), (15), (20), (31).

L. *thurberi* (Organ-pipe cactus). Brownish black spines. Nocturnal white to purplish flowers. A very slow grower. Available: (5), (14), (15), (20), (31).

Leuchtenbergia

Family: Cactaceae.

Group: Echinocactus.

Origin: Mexico.

General description: The columnar *Leuchtenbergia* grows to a maximum height of 2 feet. Its triangular-shaped, gray-green tubercles have purplish red splotches at their tips. Old tubercles have a tendency to dry up and fall off, leaving the stalk exposed at the bottom. *Leuchtenbergia* has long, weak spines.

Flower description: Yellow funnelform to bell-shaped, 4-inch flowers appear at the tips of the tubercles in the spring and summer. Flowering can be expected beginning with 3- to 4-year-old plants.

Propagation: Seed.

Culture: General cactus culture.

Recommended species: L. *principis* (Agave cactus, prism cactus). The only known species of *Leuchtenbergia*. Available: (9), (13), (15), (16), (22).

Far left: *Lithops* collection
Left: *Lobivia* hybrid

Lithops

Family: Aizoaceae.

Origin: South Africa, Southwest Africa.

General description: Lithops are members of the mesembryanthemum mimicry group. Their short, very succulent leaves imitate both the shape and coloring of rocks. They grow in stemless clumps of paired leaves approximately 1 to 2 inches in diameter.

Flower description: Yellow to white dandelion-shaped flowers emerge from between the leaves in November, December, and January. The blooms are often as large as a pair of leaves.

Propagation: Seed.

Culture: General mesembryanthemum culture. These are summer-growing plants. Water sparingly while they are growing, but withhold all water during their winter dormant period. Lithops must be in very fast-draining soil.

Recommended species: L. bella. Brownish yellow ochre coloring with green marbling; fragrant white flowers. Widely available.

L. lesliei. Gray-green skin; darker green windows marbled with rust-colored markings. Yellow-gold flowers have pale pink underside. Available: (10), (22), (31), (33), (34).

L. marmorata. Gray-green body with creamy-green mottlings in windows. White flowers. Available: (10), (22), (34).

L. verruculosa. Bluish gray skin with dark red or gray warts. Orange-brown flowers. Available: (10), (22), (34).

Since *Lithops* cross-pollinate and set seed readily in cultivation, many of the plants offered commercially are unnamed hybrids.

Lobivia

Family: Cactaceae.

Group: Echinocereus.

Origin: Bolivia, Peru, northern Argentina.

General description: Generally small, globular cacti grow as single stems or clumping mats. The green stems have ribs, sometimes tubercled, and are covered with numerous weak spines.

Flower description: Lobivias are best known for their brilliantly colored yellow, red, and purple flowers. They flower freely, and flowers are generally long lasting. The bell-shaped to short funnelform flowers appear in spring and summer.

Propagation: Seed, cuttings.

Culture: General cactus culture.

Recommended species: L. binghamiana. Yellow spines, purplish red flowers. Plants form clumps. Widely available.

Mamillopsis senilis

L. caespitosa. Clumping stems with dark spines, orange flowers. Available: (13), (16), (20), (28), (29).

L. pentlandii. Solitary stems, brownish spines, rose-colored flowers. Available: (13), (20), (28), (29).

Mamillopsis

Family: Cactaceae.
Group: Coryphantha.
Origin: Mexico.
General description: The clustering, light green stems of *Mamillopsis* are barely visible through the numerous white spines, arranged in clusters at the tip of each tubercle. Thick mats of clumping stems can cover areas up to 6 feet around, each head measuring only 2 to 3 inches in diameter.
Flower description: Red to orange funnelform flowers are borne near the tips of the stems in the spring. The blooms generally measure approximately 2 inches long and 2 inches wide.
Propagation: Seed, cuttings.
Culture: General cactus culture. Avoid overpotting.
Recommended species: M. senilis. Bristlelike, white spines. Orange-yellow flowers. Available: (5), (13), (16), (22), (29), (31).

Mammillaria

Mammillaria bocasana

Mammillaria geminispina

Family: Cactaceae.
Group: Coryphantha.
Origin: Southwestern United States, Mexico, Central America, and northern South America.
General description: The numerous and wonderfully diverse members of the genus *Mammillaria* grow in globular- to cylindrical-shaped stems. Often these are clumping, but sometimes they remain solitary or become procumbent. Specimen sizes can range from tiny individual heads only a few inches wide to massive clumps several feet across. Tubercles are arranged in spiraling rows. *Mammillaria* is distinguished from the closely related genus *Coryphantha* by the lack of grooves in the tubercle tips and the location of the flowers at the base of the tubercle in *Mammillaria*. The widely varied and distinctive spines come in all shapes, colors, sizes, textures, and arrangements. They are largely responsible for the mammillaria's attractiveness.
Flower description: Small bell-shaped flowers come in many colors— white to cream, reds, pinks, and yellows. Unlike other cacti, whose flowers are borne on areoles, mammillaria blooms arise from the joints of tubercles in a ring around the top of the plant. Blossoming occurs from March to October.
Propagation: Seed. Unrooted offsets can be removed and potted up.
Culture: General cactus culture. Except for *Rebutia*, *Mammillaria* is the easiest cactus genus to grow and flower. Soil for very small species or plants with big taproots should be especially porous. *Mammillaria* species require generous watering during spring and summer. They can withstand temperatures to near freezing if kept dry during the winter. Woolly varieties should be watered carefully to avoid rot in the soft spines.
Recommended species: M. bocasana 'Inermis' (Snowball cactus). Many hooked, yellowish spines. Yellow or pink flowers. Available: (5), (13), (16), (18), (20), (22), (28), (31).

M. camptotricha (*M. albescens*). Bristly, yellowish spines. Greenish white flowers. Available: (13), (15), (16), (20), (28), (31).

M. collinsii. Widely available.

M. columbiana. Solitary cylindrical stems. Deep pink flowers. Widely available.

M. compressa. Woolly axils. Bristly white spines. Purplish red flowers. Widely available.

M. elegans. Cylindrical stems with many needle-shaped white spines. Red flowers. Available: (5), (13), (15), (16), (22).

M. geminispina. Woolly white axils and soft white spines. Carmine flowers. Available: (5), (9), (13), (16), (22).

M. hemisphaerica. (See: *M. heyderi.*)

M. heyderi (Coral cactus). Brown-tipped white spines. Flowers white with red or pink. Available: (2), (13), (16), (18), (20), (23).

M. magnimamma. Black-tipped, curved spines. Cream-white flowers. Widely available.

M. prolifera (Little-candles, silver cluster cactus). Small, globe-shaped, with bristly white spines. Yellowish flowers. Available: (13), (16), (20), (22), (24), (31).

M. schiedeana. Cylindrical, with many bristly, yellow-tipped white spines. Widely available.

M. zeilmanniana (Rose-pincushion). Solitary stems, purple flowers. Widely available.

Melocactus

Family: Cactaceae.
Group: Cactus.
Origin: Caribbean Islands and tropical America.
General description: The prominently ribbed, medium to dark green, oblong stems reach a maximum 18-inch diameter, 36-inch height, depending upon species. Clusters of yellow, reddish brown, or nearly black spines are located along the ribs. The melocactus is best noted for its cephalium, a densely woolly growth produced at the top of the plant after the stem has reached its mature size.
Flower description: Tiny red, pink, or purplish flowers are borne on the cephalium during spring and summer. It takes a plant from 5 to 20 years to reach maturity, develop a cephalium, and come into bloom.
Propagation: Seed.
Culture: This shallow-rooted plant requires a shallow container and a loose, very well-drained soil. Feed frequently but very sparingly in summer. Cut down on water in winter. Specimens grown from seed are generally less temperamental and sensitive to cold.
Recommended species: *M. bahiensis.* Straight brown spines. Low cephalium. Pinkish flowers. Native to Brazil. Available: (13), (15), (16), (21), (31).

M. intortus (Turk's-cap cactus). Large, growing to 3 feet high. Long cephalium. Pinkish flowers. Grows throughout the Caribbean islands. Available: (13), (15), (20), (31).

M. matanzanus. Miniature variety, maximum 4 inches high. Matures in 4 to 5 years. Native of Cuba. Easiest to grow of the genus. Available: (2), (5), (13), (15), (16).

Myrtillocactus

Family: Cactaceae.
Group: Cereus.
Origin: Mexico.
General description: Tall, stout, branching stems often grow to a maximum height of 20 feet in habitat. Its blue-green stems have 5 to 8 ribs and black spines.
Flower description: Clusters of small white flowers are borne on the areoles in spring and summer.
Propagation: Seed, cuttings.
Culture: General cactus culture. Young plants can be kept in containers. Mature specimens make dramatic landscape accents.
Recommended species: *M. geometrizans* (Blue-candle, blue-flame). The only species currently listed. Available: (9), (13), (15), (16).

Melocactus bahiensis

Myrtillocactus geometrizans

Neobesseya missouriensis

Neobesseya

Family: Cactaceae.

Group: Coryphantha.

Origin: Missouri River basin, from North Dakota to Texas.

General description: Generally considered a subgenus of *Coryphantha*, *Neobesseya* is characterized by dull green, clumping, globular stems divided into irregular tubercles. While the clumps of stems can grow to be very large, individual heads seldom exceed 2 inches in diameter. *Neobesseya* has semistiff, 1-inch-long, brownish spines.

Flower description: The 2-inch-long, funnelform blooms have pale yellow inner petals, and a beautiful fringe of brownish green petals on the outside. They appear at the apex of the plant in spring. The fruits take a full year to mature.

Propagation: Seed.

Culture: General cactus culture. Recommended for more experienced growers; *Neobesseya* is frequently difficult to establish.

Recommended species: N. missouriensis (*Coryphantha missouriensis*). The only species. Available: (13), (20), (22), (31).

Neochilenia

Family: Cactaceae.

Group: Echinocactus.

Origin: Chile.

General description: Like the closely related *Neoporteria*, members of this genus are globular to cylindrical plants, reaching a maximum height of 10 inches. The stems are often dark purple-brown, tubercled, and armed with many short brown spines.

Flower description: The bell-shaped, purple-red and green flowers measure 1¼ to 2 inches long. They appear near the top of the stems in spring and summer.

Propagation: Seed, occasionally by offsets.

Culture: General cactus culture. Moderately easy to grow.

Recommended species: N. aerocarpa (*N. fulva* 'Aerocarpa'). Available: (5), (8), (13), (29).

N. napina. Spiraling tubercles. Black spines. Yellow flowers. Available: (5), (8), (13), (23), (26), (29), (31).

N. wagenknechtii 'Multiflora'. Available: (5), (8), (20), (29).

Neochilenia napina

Neoporteria

Family: Cactaceae.

Group: Echinocactus.

Origin: Chile to Peru.

General description: The green, short, cylindrical stems of neoporteria are covered with many spines. The ribs have separate tubercles. The entire plant grows to a maximum height of 10 inches.

Flower description: Pinkish, bell-shaped flowers measure 1½ inches long, are borne several at a time from one areole in December, January, and February.

Propagation: Seed.

Culture: General cactus culture. These winter bloomers need generous culture from November to March. They require a rest period during spring and summer.

Recommended species: N. nidus (*N. gerocephala*, *N. senilis*). Densely covered with curved, white, needle-shaped spines. Pink flowers. Widely available.

N. subgibbosa. Many needle-shaped, brownish spines. Pink or red flowers. Available: (15), (16), (20), (23), (29), (31).

Neoporteria subgibbosa

Far left: *Notocactus haselbergii*
Left: *Opuntia microdasys* 'Albispina'

Notocactus

Family: Cactaceae.
Group: Echinocactus.
Origin: Brazil, Argentina, Paraguay.
General description: The dark green, globe-shaped to cylindrical stems of *Notocactus* have rounded ribs and grow to a height of 10 inches, although some species can reach 6 feet. Some species are covered with fine white spines; others have sharp, stiff, yellowish to brown spines.
Flower description: Most plants have yellow flowers, a few red-purple. In general, they are bell-shaped, measuring from 1 to 3 inches, appearing at the apex of the cactus in the summer.
Propagation: Seed.
Culture: General cactus culture. An easy-to-grow cactus, good for beginners.
Recommended species: N. apricus. Short and globe-shaped, 15 to 20 ribs, with 3-inch-long yellow flowers. Forms clumps. Available: (5), (13), (15), (16), (22).

N. graessneri. Solitary, thick stems with needle-shaped, glassy-yellow spines, 60 or more ribs. Yellowish green flowers. Available: (5), (8), (20), (23), (24), (28).

N. haselbergii (Scarlet barrel cactus). Globular stems, 5 inches thick, with 30 or more ribs. Orange to red flowers bloom from January to February. Widely available.

N. ottonis. Single stems or small clumps, with 10 to 13 ribs. Needle-shaped, yellow or brown spines. Yellow flowers. Widely available.

Opuntia microdasys

Opuntia

Family: Cactaceae.
Group: Opuntia.
Origin: Massachusetts to the southern tip of South America.
General description: This large and varied genus is characterized by three different sizes and shapes of stems: flat, oval pads to 12 inches across; long, thin stems to 4 or 5 feet in length; or small, globular stems to 3 inches in diameter. The skin is generally green, although a few species are purple. Spination on pad-shaped leaves is usually a cluster of straight spines, bristly to stout, dotted across the surface. Very small, easily detached, barbed spines called glochids are the source of the common name "prickly pear." Tubular and globular plants have varied spine sizes and arrangements.
Flower description: Large, bell-shaped flowers range in color, from mostly yellow to orange, or purple, or white. On pad-shaped species, they are on the circumference of the stems. Tubular and globular species bear their flowers from areoles.
Propagation: Seed, cuttings.

Pachyphytum hybrid

Culture: Many opuntias are cold-hardy, and can be used in the landscape in most parts of the U.S.

Recommended species: O. basilaris (Beaver-tail). Gray-green to purplish pads. Flowers purple to rose, yellow, or rarely white. Available: (4), (13), (16), (17).

O. humifusa (*O. compressa*). Flat pads 2 to 6 inches long, forms spreading clumps. Flowers yellow. Hardy in the North. Available: (4), (13).

O. microdasys (Rabbit-ears, bunny-ears). Yellowish green pads with tufts of yellow spines. Yellow flowers. 'Albispina' (Polka-dot cactus): tufts of white spines. 'Rufida' (Cinnamon cactus, red bunny-ears): tufts of red spines. All widely available.

Oreocereus

See: Borzicactus

Pachyphytum

Family: Crassulaceae.

Origin: Mexico.

General description: The fat, rounded leaves of pachyphytum form attractive rosettes on long, succulent stems. Leaf color can range from a dusty gray-pink to glaucous blue. The diameter of each rosette can be up to 8 inches across, depending on species.

Flower description: Small, bell-shaped flowers are borne on a pendant stalk in spring and summer. Color ranges from white to orange to red or pink.

Propagation: Cuttings, seed.

Culture: General succulent culture. *Pachyphytum* species need plenty of bright—but not burning—sun to bring out maximum leaf color. Their long stems make them good hanging-basket subjects.

Recommended species: P. 'Blue Haze'. Thickly succulent, bluish leaves. Available: (18), (20), (21), (24), (35), (36).

P. compactum (Thick plant). Rounded, very succulent leaves, whitish with a nearly lavender hue. Available: (18), (20), (21), (22), (24), (31).

Pachypodium

Family: Apocynaceae.

Origin: South Africa, Angola, Madagascar.

General description: This widely varied genus includes plants that are shrubby, have tuberous root systems, or are columnar and covered with thorns, similar to cacti. The species with tuberous root systems and those with thickened trunks are generally those most sought after by succulent collectors. Most species have long, thin, leathery, dark green, deciduous foliage.

Flower description: Flowers of *Pachypodium* range from white to yellow to red. The star-shaped blooms, borne at the tips of the branches, measure up to 2 inches across, appearing in the spring.

Propagation: Seed.

Pachypodium species

Culture: General succulent culture. In winter, *Pachypodium* plants go through a leafless dormancy—water should be withheld. The tuberous rootstocks of certain species make them excellent "bonsai" subjects.

Recommended species: P. lealii. Tuberous, club-shaped trunk with treelike branches that carry small leaves, stout spines. White flowers. Available: (7), (9), (15), (25), (31), (33).

P. lameri. Spiny succulent trunk can grow to 6 feet high or more. Easy for the beginner. Widely available.

P. rosulatum. Short, thick caudex branching into spiny arms, topped by foliage rosette. Bright yellow flowers on long stalk. Available: (7), (9), (15), (33).

P. windsorii. (*P. baronii* var. *windsorii*). Dwarf caudex covered with rough skin and tiny spines. Red flowers. Available: (7), (9), (15), (33).

× *Pachyveria*

Family: Crassulaceae.

Origin: Hybrid of *Echeveria* × *Pachyphytum*.

General description: These products of bigeneric crosses between *Echeveria* and *Pachyphytum* have produced plants with the best characteristics of both parents. × *Pachyveria* hybrids have the perfect rosette form of *Echeveria* and stunning color range of *Pachyphytum*. The rosettes of succulent, glaucous leaves grow on rather long, succulent stems. Colors vary widely, including many shades of pink and luminous blues, grays, lavenders, and greens.

Flower description: Like its parents, × *Pachyveria* bears its bell-shaped flowers on a pendant stalk, mainly in spring and summer. Colors include yellow, orange, pink, and red.

Propagation: Cuttings.

Culture: General succulent culture.

Recommended species: × *P. glauca*. Rosettes of glaucous leaves measuring to 4 inches across. Available: (20), (24).

× *P. haagei* (Jewel plant). Rosettes of bluish green leaves with purplish red at pointed tips. Available: (21), (22).

× *Pachyveria* hybrid

Parodia

Family: Cactaceae.

Group: Echinocactus.

Origin: Argentina, Bolivia, Paraguay, Brazil.

General description: Small, globular to cylindrical, light green stems are usually solitary, occasionally clustering. They grow to a maximum 3 inches in diameter, 10 inches in height, with ribs that are divided into spiraling tubercles. *Parodia* has many yellowish to red-brown spines.

Flower description: Brightly colored yellow to red flowers are borne in the yellowish wool at the plant's apex during the summer. Blooms are generally wide funnelform shape, measuring 1 to 2 inches long.

Propagation: Seed.

Culture: General cactus culture. Prevent accumulation of water at the collar of the plant. *Parodia* roots need an open, nourishing soil and even moisture during the growing season.

Recommended species: P. *aureispina* (Tom-thumb). Globe-shaped stems with bristly white spines. Yellow flowers. Available: (2), (13), (15), (16), (22).

P. *maassii*. Solitary oval stems. Yellowish spines. Red flowers. Available: (16), (20), (28), (29), (31).

P. *mutabilis*. Many bristly white spines with stouter red to orange spines. Yellow flowers. Available: (16), (20), (22), (28), (31).

Parodia maassii

Pelargonium

Family: Geraniaceae.

Origin: South Africa, Madagascar.

General description: The species most interesting to collectors have succulent, dark green stems sometimes armed with spines. Foliage is relatively sparse, green, and lacy-edged.

Flower description: Clusters of flowers resembling the genus' most popular members, the common geraniums, appear on thin stems at the plant's tips. Colors range from white to pink, red, and purple; petals usually have darker markings. Flowering time is in spring and summer.

Propagation: Cuttings, seed.

Culture: General succulent culture. Species with thinner stems are generally easier to grow.

Pelargonium species

Pelecyphora asseliformis

Recommended species: P. echinatum (Cactus geranium, sweetheart geranium). The easiest-to-grow succulent pelargonium. Available: (13), (16), (35), (36).

Pelecyphora

Family: Cactaceae.
Group: Echinocactus.
Origin: Mexico.
General description: The green, tubercled stems of *Pelecyphora* grow either singly or in mat-forming clumps. They are globular to club-shaped (wider at the top than bottom). A distinctive feature of these cacti is their spinal arrangement. Elongated areoles are surrounded by short, white spines that are parallel with the plant's surface.
Flower description: Short, tubular flowers are borne on the spine clusters below the top of the plant. The rose- to violet-colored flowers open during the day, close at night in the spring and summer. They measure up to 1¼ inches across.
Propagation: Seed, cuttings.
Culture: General cactus culture.
Recommended species: P. asseliformis (Hatchet cactus). Columnar, club-shaped stems to 4 inches high. Rose-colored flowers. Available: (2), (13), (16), (22), (28), (29), (31).
P. strobiliformis. Depressed globular stems to 1½ inches high. Light to dark magenta flowers. Available: (13), (22), (31).

Pleiospilos

Family: Aizoaceae.
Origin: South Africa.
General description: Thick, succulent, low-growing leaf pairs resemble small rocks. These mesembryanthemum mimicry plants are brown-gray, with darker-colored dots over the skin. They grow in stemless clumps that range in size from 1 to 5 inches in diameter.
Flower description: Yellow-orange, dandelionlike flowers emerge from between the leaves in the summer. Blossoms are usually 2 to 3 inches across.
Propagation: Seed.
Culture: General mesembryanthemum culture. Though more challenging than many succulents, *Pleiospilos* is generally easier to grow than most mesembryanthemums.
Recommended species: P. bolusii (Mimicry plant, living-rock cactus). Gray-green or brownish skin with many dark green dots. Bright yellow flowers. Available: (5), (7), (13), (16), (18), (36).
P. nelii (Splitrock, cleftstone). Dark gray-green or reddish leaves. Salmon pink-yellow flowers. Available: (5), (7), (13), (16), (18).

Pleiospilos species

Portulacaria

Family: Portulaceae.
Origin: South Africa.
General description: A monotypic shrub, with reddish brown trunk and stems and small, succulent, green leaves.
Flower description: Clusters of small, pale pink flowers are produced by very old specimens. Younger plants do not flower.
Propagation: Cuttings.
Culture: General succulent culture. Very easy to grow. The attractive, reddish brown stems and shrubby habit make *Portulacaria* an ideal "bonsai" specimen.
Recommended species: P. afra (Elephant bush). Green leaves. 'Variegata' has light green and creamy white variegated foliage. Both are widely available in catalogs and retail nurseries.

Portulacaria afra 'Variegata'

Puya

Family: Bromeliaceae.

Origin: Andes Mountains of South America, Costa Rica.

General description: All of the species of *Puya* are rugged, high-altitude plants. Most are stemless or short-stemmed plants 2 to 6 feet in diameter. The stiff basal leaves surround a tall flower spike that can reach 12 feet or taller. Older plants will form clumps up to 25 feet in diameter.

Flower description: The narrow bell-shaped flowers come in iridescent blue, green, and purple surrounded by equally colorful bracts in pink, red, or brown. Tall flower spikes may carry hundreds of individual flowers. In the garden, the flowers are constantly visited by hummingbirds.

Propagation: Seed, cuttings.

Culture: General succulent culture, although they will respond favorably to richer soil and more water.

Recommended species: P. alpestris. The narrow leaves with hooked spines along their edges reach 2 to 3 feet in length. The 3-foot flower spike bears a mass of iridescent blue-green flowers. Older plants form clumps. Available: (1).

P. chilensis. Similar to *P. alpestris* but larger. Leaves can be 4 to 5 feet long and all parts of the plant proportionately larger. Forms large clumps. Flowers are a metallic greenish yellow on 12-foot spikes. Available: (1).

Rebutia

Family: Cactaceae.

Group: Lobivia.

Origin: Argentina, Bolivia, Paraguay.

General description: Rebutia species are small, globe-shaped, light green to dark shiny green cacti covered with many small, wartlike tubercles. The short spines range from white to dark brown.

Flower description: Large yellow, red, or purple flowers make this genus a popular collector's item. From 5 to 20 very long, thin, funnelform flowers open from the base of the plant during summer, often obscuring the cactus itself.

Propagation: Seed and offsets.

Culture: General cactus culture. These free-blooming cacti are good for beginners. They remain small enough to fit the narrowest windowsill. Rebutias prefer filtered sun.

Recommended species: R. deminuta. Brown-tipped or brown spines. Large, dark orange-red flowers. Available: (13), (16), (18), (28).

R. grandiflora (Scarlet crown cactus). Crimson flowers to 2½ inches long. Available: (13), (16), (21), (24), (28).

R. krainziana. Woolly areoles, white spines. Red to crimson flowers. Available: (5), (8), (15), (16), (22).

R. kupperana. Radial brown spines. Orange-red flowers. Available: (13), (15), (16), (18), (28).

R. minuscula (Red-crown). Bristly white spines. Crimson flowers. Widely available.

R. senilis (Fire-crown cactus). Carmine-red flowers. Widely available.

Rhipsalis

Family: Cactaceae.

Group: Cereus.

Origin: Tropical America.

General description: The jointed, branching, leafless stems of *Rhipsalis* cascade or climb in their native habitat. These epiphytes have aerial roots on their flattened or cylindrical green stems. They are generally spineless; a few species have insignificant bristles at the areoles.

Rebutia hybrid

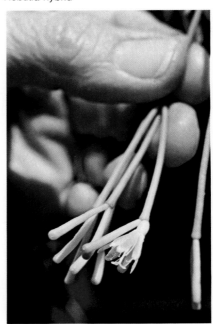

Rhipsalis capilliformis

Rhipsalis species

Flower description: Flower shape, color, and size vary greatly within the genus. Some species have lovely, small, bell-shaped blossoms ranging from white to red; many have tiny, nondescript flowers whose yellowish greens blend in with the stems. The fruits are small, nearly transparent berries that greatly resemble milk-glass beads.

Propagation: Cuttings, seed.

Culture: General tropical cactus culture. *Rhipsalis* is particularly well suited to hanging-basket culture.

Recommended species: R. capilliformis. Thin, jointed, branching green stems (see photograph page 16). Small cream-colored flowers. Available: (11), (22), (30), (35).

Schlumbergera

Family: Cactaceae.

Group: Hylocereus.

Origin: Brazil.

General description: The flat, jointed stems of this genus have scalloped edges and short, inconspicuous bristles. The stems grow in segments, forming a sort of chain from the plant's trunk.

Flower description: Schlumbergeras are cultivated for their numerous winter flowers. The hooded blossoms come in bright shades of purple, red, pink, and white. They are borne on the ends of the jointed stems.

Propagation: Cuttings, seed.

Culture: General tropical cactus culture. The schlumbergera's winter bloom cycle requires more water during November to March, tapering off April through September. They make ideal hanging-basket specimens and do well as houseplants.

Recommended species: S. bridgesii (Christmas cactus). Cerise flowers on stems to 1 inch long. Widely available in retail nurseries and through catalogs.

S. truncata (Thanksgiving cactus, crab cactus). Similar to *S. bridgesii,* but with scallop-edged stems, irregular flowers. Widely available in retail nurseries and through catalogs.

Many new cultivars extend the color range and bloom period.

Sedum

Family: Crassulaceae.

Origin: Northern temperate regions, parts of Africa and South America.

General description: Very few generalizations can be made about this

Below: *Schlumbergera bridgesii*
Below right: *Sedum × rubrotinctum*

large, varied genus. The succulent foliage comes in many colors and forms, including vining, creeping, and upright shrubby growth.

Flower description: Sedums produce small flowers in colors ranging from white and yellow to dusty pink or deep rose. The small blossoms generally cluster on a short stem above the foliage.

Propagation: Cuttings, seed.

Culture: General succulent culture. Sedums are among the easiest to grow of the succulent genera. Many species and varieties are cold-hardy, making them excellent outdoor plants in cold-winter regions.

Recommended species: S. morganianum (Donkey's-tail). Succulent, light green leaves cluster on hanging stems. Frost-tender. Widely available.

S. oxypetalum. Shrubby plant, to 5 feet tall. The bark on its trunk peels. Reddish flowers appear after leaves drop. Widely available.

S. × rubrotinctum (Christmas-cheer). Small, very succulent leaves on short stems. Light green foliage becomes red when grown in full sun. A good ground cover in frost-free areas. Widely available.

S. sieboldii. Hardy ground cover with abundant fall flowers. Widely available.

S. spathulifolium. Rosettes of tiny dark green outer leaves with grayish inner leaves on short, draping stems. An attractive container plant or ground cover. Some cultivars winter hardy in the North. Widely available.

S. spectabile. Hardy succulent for the perennial border. Cultivars available in many variations of foliage and flower color. Widely available.

Selenicereus

Family: Cactaceae.

Group: Hylocereus.

Origin: Caribbean Islands, tropical America.

General description: Climbing or hanging stems can measure up to 15 feet long. They are slender (½ to 1½ inches thick), cylindrical, green when young, turning purple as they age. Depending upon the species, some stems are tubular, others ribbed or angular. Short, bristly spines are borne in clusters on the areoles of most species. The stems produce aerial roots, intended for grasping the trees that *Selenicereus* climbs in its native habitat.

Flower description: Large funnelform flowers are borne along the stems. The white blossoms measure up to 8 inches long, to 10 inches across. The summer flowers open in the evenings.

Propagation: Seed, cuttings.

Culture: General tropical cactus culture. Due to its vigorous climbing growth habit, *Selenicereus* must be given adequate room. Well suited to hanging-basket culture.

Recommended species: S. grandiflorus (Queen-of-the-night). Ribbed stems. White flowers 7 to 10 inches long. Widely available.

S. pteranthus (Princess-of-the-night). Prominently ribbed stems. Fragrant flowers, 10 to 12 inches long. Available: (9), (18), (21), (22).

Sempervivum

Family: Crassulaceae.

Origin: Mountains of Europe, western Asia, and North Africa.

General description: This large genus is characterized by small, rosette-shaped plants that grow in mat-forming clumps. The nearly stemless leaves have pointed ends and come in a vast array of colors, including every shade of green and some very dramatic reds and purples. The succulent rosettes seldom exceed 3 inches across and are often covered with small hairs, sometimes numerous enough to give the appearance of spider webs.

Flower description: The flower color in *Sempervivum* varies widely. The small flowers are borne on a stalk that pushes out of the rosette's center in spring or summer.

Schlumbergera hybrid

Sedum morganianum

Selenicereus hybrid

Sempervivum tectorum

Top: *Senecio rowleyanus*
Above: *Senecio haworthii*

Propagation: Cuttings, division, seed.

Culture: General succulent culture. *Sempervivum* species are easy to grow and have an extra advantage—many species and cultivars are winter-hardy. They can be planted outdoors in cold-winter areas with minimal protection.

Recommended species: S. arachnoideum (Cobweb houseleek). Tiny, dense rosettes of green leaves with many fine hairs. Bright red flowers. Widely available.

S. 'Clara Noyes'. Lovely rosettes of deep red, succulent leaves. Available: (15), (19), (29).

S. tectorum (Common houseleek). Widely opened, green rosette, often tipped with purple. Widely available.

Senecio

Family: Compositae.

Origin: Worldwide.

General description: This large and widely varied genus includes species whose growth habits range from small succulents, to hanging or climbing vines, to large shrubs. The white-felted, green, or bluish green stems of the succulent species are spineless. Leaves are spherical, thickly succulent, or flat and elongated.

Flower description: Small daisylike flowers come in orange, yellow, white, or red, depending upon species. All are small, seldom exceeding 1 inch across. They are borne at the ends of the stems in summer.

Propagation: Cuttings, seed.

Culture: General succulent culture. Very easy to grow.

Recommended species: S. haworthii (Cocoon plant). Small succulent shrub with soft, feltlike hairs on leaves. Yellow-orange flowers. Available: (7), (15), (22), (31), (36).

S. herreianus (Gooseberry kleinia). Hanging or climbing vine with thickly succulent, elliptical green leaves. Excellent hanging-basket specimen. Available: (13), (15), (16), (22), (29), (31), (35), (36).

S. rowleyanus (String-of-beads). Spherical green leaves on hanging or climbing vine. A beautiful hanging-basket subject. Widely available.

Setiechinopsis

Family: Cactaceae.

Group: Cereus.

Origin: Argentina.

General description: A monotypic, small, ribbed cactus characterized by solitary, slender stems to 1 inch in diameter, 6 inches long. Each stem has 11 ribs and short, bristly, brown spines.

Flower description: White flowers, measuring 2 inches across, are borne on a very long, thin tube from the top of the plant. Blooming occurs in late spring and summer.

Propagation: Seed.

Culture: General cactus culture. A good container plant.

Recommended species: S. mirabilis. Available: (15), (16), (23), (29), (31).

Stapelia

Family: Asclepiadaceae.

Origin: Africa, Asia.

General description: Stapelia stems are from ½ to 1 inch in diameter, 4 to 12 inches long, and grow in clusters to 2 feet in diameter, depending on species. The gray-green to dark brownish green stems are leafless, but have soft teeth on their margins.

Flower description: Stapelias are grown for their large (1 to 5 inches across), 5-lobed, starfish-shaped flowers. The showy blossoms—generally yellowish, splotched with maroon or brown—are borne along the stems.

Setiechinopsis mirabilis

Blooming occurs from summer to autumn, each flower lasting approximately 2 days. The flowers are carrion-scented as a means of attracting the flies that pollinate them. Therefore, stapelias are best grown in a place where the beautiful flowers can be seen but not smelled.

Propagation: Seed, offsets, cuttings.

Culture: General stapeliad culture. *Stapelia* species need very loose, porous soil. They will rot if kept too wet and will be attacked by mealybugs if too dry. They benefit from frequent repotting. Water very sparingly in cold weather. Not recommended for beginners.

Recommended species: S. hirsuta (Hairy toad plant). Cream or yellowish and dark purple-brown flowers. Available: (9), (13), (16), (18), (20), (22), (24), (33).

S. pasadenensis. Wine-red flowers. Available: (7), (16), (18), (22).

S. verrucosa. Flowers are pale yellow spotted with blood-red. Available: (7), (13), (16), (20), (22).

Stapelia pasadenensis

Strombocactus

Family: Cactaceae.

Group: Echinocactus.

Origin: Mexico.

General description: The round, disclike stems of *Strombocactus* are made up of irregularly shaped tubercles that range in color from blue-gray to blue-green to gray-green. Wider than high, slow-growing, and always solitary, the *Strombocactus* species seldom exceed a 1- to 3-inch diameter or grow taller than 1 inch. Most species have weak straight or curved spines in clusters on the areoles. A few develop hair or wool.

Flower description: Measuring ½ to 1½ inches across, the short-tubed, wide-funnelform flowers are large in proportion to the plant. They are white with purple markings and appear at the center of the cactus in late summer.

Propagation: Seed.

Culture: General cactus culture. Best if grown in a container, but avoid overpotting. Winter watering must be very light.

Recommended species: S. pseudomacrochele (Turbinicarpus pseudomacrochele). Stiff, twisted gray spines. Available: (15), (16), (28), (31).

S. schmiedickeanus (Turbinicarpus schmiedickeanus). Curved brown spines. Rose-colored flowers. Available: (5), (8), (15), (16).

Strombocactus species

Sulcorebutia

Family: Cactaceae.

Group: Lobivia.

Origin: South America.

General description: The globular, tubercled stems of *Sulcorebutia* are generally small growers, seldom exceeding 2 to 3 inches in diameter. They cluster as the plants mature. *Sulcorebutia* species are most easily distinguished from *Rebutia* by their elongated areoles and short, recurved spines.

Flower description: Large, funnelform flowers appear in spring and early summer. Their colors range from bright yellows and deep gold to red and orange. While *Rebutia* produces flowers only from the base of the stems, *Sulcorebutia* flowers can be produced on any of the lower areoles.

Propagation: Seed, cuttings.

Culture: General cactus culture. These petite, colorful flowering cacti make ideal windowsill specimens.

Recommended species: S. caniguerallii. Approximately 1-inch-diameter heads with very dark brownish green stems and very short comblike spines. Reddish flowers with yellow throat. Available: (31), (36).

S. crispata. Spherical heads to 2 inches in diameter. Light green body, curly honey-colored spines to ¼ inch long. Bright pink flowers. Available: (31), (36).

Sulcorebutia species

Thelocactus nidulans

S. glomeriseta. Deep green body to 2 inches in diameter with black spines. Flowers of brilliant cerise. Available: (31), (36).

Thelocactus

Family: Cactaceae.
Group: Coryphantha.
Origin: Mexico.
General description: Thelocactus is characterized by small-growing, depressed, globular, or occasionally cylindrical stems, most measuring under 7 inches high. The bright green to gray-green stems are divided into tubercles that, in some instances, are united to form ribs. Spines range in color from brown and gray to white, yellow, and red, and are clustered at the tubercle tips.
Flower description: Wide open, bell-shaped flowers are borne on the top of the plant, in colors ranging from yellow to red-pink. Flowering occurs in spring.
Propagation: Seed.
Culture: General cactus culture. These plants grow best under slightly drier than average culture, and in a soil mix that includes a little gypsum.
Recommended species: T. bicolor (Glory-of-Texas). Purple flowers on conical stems. Available: (2), (9), (13), (16).
T. leucacanthus. Clustering stems with yellow to gray spines, yellow flowers. Available: (13), (16), (23), (28), (31).
T. nidulans. Solitary stems with brown spines, yellowish white flowers. Available: (9), (16), (24), (28).

Tillandsia

Family: Bromeliaceae.
Origin: Tropical America.
General description: The long, curving spindle- to triangular-shaped leaves of *Tillandsia* form a rosette, occasionally with a stem. These epiphytes have aerial roots for gripping trees, rock cliffs, or similar support in their native habitat. Unlike succulents, they do not store water in their stems and leaves; they survive on what little moisture is borne through the air. The foliage is often an attractive silvery color, with highlights of pink to pale orange.
Flower description: Clusters of small blue, green, purple, red, orange, or white flowers are borne on a stalk.
Propagation: Division, seed.

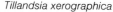

Tillandsia xerographica

Culture: Dry-growing *Tillandsia* species are best mounted on a piece of plain wood, cork bark, or tree fern trunk (available from specialty nurseries). Plants should be misted in warm, dry weather to ensure adequate moisture.
Recommended species: T. ionantha. Dwarf rosette of green outer leaves, pink or red inner leaves. Violet flowers. Available: (1), (6), (12), (17), (32), (35).
T. usneoides (Spanish moss). Many-branched, leafy, hanging stems. Silvery gray. Common in the southern United States. Available: (1), (32).

Trichocereus

Family: Cactaceae.
Group: Cereus.
Origin: Andes Mountains, from Chile and northwestern Argentina through Bolivia and Peru to Ecuador.
General description: Members of this genus range from plants with tall, branching, columnar stems to procumbent, creeping cacti that can stretch as far as 20 or 30 feet. The prominently ribbed green stems have clusters of stout yellow-brown or gray spines along their ribs.

Far left: *Trichodiadema bulbosum*
Left: *Trichocereus* hybrid

Flower description: Most species have large, fragrant, white, funnelform flowers. Blooms measuring up to 8 inches across open from areoles all along the stems in summer.

Propagation: Seed, cuttings.

Culture: General cactus culture. These cacti make good landscape specimens in frost-free areas, tolerating greater than average water and low-nitrogen fertilizers.

Recommended species: T. pachanoi. Tall, upright, branching stems to 20 feet. Fragrant white flowers. Available: (13), (16), (20), (23), (25).

T. spachianus (Torch cactus). Upright stems branching at the base, to 3 feet high. Fragrant white flowers. Widely available.

Trichodiadema

Family: Aizoaceae.

Origin: South Africa, Ethiopia.

General description: Members of this genus tend to grow as shrubby or short-stemmed succulents. The longer-stemmed plants are often used as ground covers in frost-free areas. The shorter-stemmed species have thick, tuberous roots. All species have small, spindle-shaped, green to gray-green leaves with small, spinelike bristles at their tops.

Flower description: Small daisylike flowers appear in early summer near the end of the stems. Their colors include bright magenta, brilliant reddish purple, white, and yellow.

Propagation: Seed, cuttings.

Culture: General succulent culture. Most growth occurs in summer. Plants respond well to diluted applications of low-nitrogen fertilizer and frequent pruning. Tuberous-rooted plants make excellent "bonsai" subjects with the upper portion of the roots exposed.

Recommended species: T. bulbosum. Light tan, thick, tuberous roots. Magenta flowers. Available: (13), (16), (20), (22).

T. densum. Tuberous roots. Tiny, succulent, green stems. Carmine flowers. Widely available.

Turbinicarpus

See: Strombocactus.

Yucca

Family: Agavaceae.

Origin: Western United States to Central America.

General description: Stiff sword-shaped leaves grow in terminal rosettes on stemless or short-trunked plants. A few species are treelike in size and appearance. In many species the leaves are stiff and carry a sharp terminal spine.

Flower description: Flowers are borne on a tall spike in dense heads. Most flowers are white or tinged with purple.

Propagation: Seed, cuttings.

Culture: General succulent culture but plants will respond well to a richer soil and more water.

Recommended species: Y. elephantipes. Leaves 4 feet long and 3 inches wide hang gracefully from a trunk which can grow to 30 feet in height. Older plants branch readily and are quite treelike. Widely available.

Y. filamentosa (Adam's needle). Nearly stemless plant with narrow leaves to 2½ feet long. Forms large clumps. The flower spike is straight and can be as tall as 15 feet although most are much shorter. Hardy in the north. Widely available.

Mail-Order Sources

Here you will find a list of mail-order nurseries. They made it convenient for collectors all over the United States and Canada to buy a wide variety of high-quality plants. These mail-order nurseries, and the informative catalogs they provide, are a real help to collectors who do not have the advantage of a nearby nursery or garden center. On the whole, they are general succulent nurseries. If they specialize in one genus or another, their specialty is noted below the address.

Succulents received from mail-order nurseries often arrive potted in lightweight soil mixes specially prepared for shipping and handling. The soil mix is adequate to maintain the plant during the shipping process, but some plants may need to be repotted in another rooting medium before they become a part of your permanent collection. For complete information on potting, see "Basic Care and Propagation," starting on page 22.

One final note: the mail-order nurseries are numbered from 1 to 37. These numbers correspond to the numbers that appear in the encyclopedia (pages 92–138) after the recommended species. Catalog availability on recommended species is indicated, except for those that are widely available.

Mail-order nurseries

The following is a list of 37 mail-order nurseries. Most of them have a large selection of both cacti and other succulents. Specialization in one or two genera or families has been noted below the nursery's name and address.

Seaborn del Dios Nursery (1)
Route 3, P.O. Box 455
Escondido, CA 92025
Specializes in bromeliads and cycads.

Barnet Cactus Garden (2)
1104 Meadowview Drive
Bossier City, LA 71111

Desert Dan's (3)
Nursery Seed Company
Minitola, NJ 08341

Intermountain Cactus (4)
1478 North 750 East
Kaysville, UT 84037
Specializes in opuntias and other winter-hardy plants.

Modlins Cactus Gardens (5)
2416 El Corto
Vista, CA 92083

Nature's Curiosity Shop (6)
2560 Ridgeway Drive
National City, CA 92050
Has a large selection of succulents and bromeliads.

Kirkpatrick's Rare & Unusual Cactus (7)
27785 De Anza Street
Barstow, CA 92311
Offers a very large selection of unusual cacti and other succulents.

Howard Wise (8)
3710 June Street
San Bernardino, CA 92405
Deals exclusively in cacti.

Helen's Cactus (9)
2205 Mirasol Avenue
Brownsville, TX 78520

Collector's Succulents (10)
Cathryn Mangold
P.O. Box 1998
Rancho Santa Fe, CA 92067

California Epi Center (11)
P. O. Box 2474
Van Nuys, CA 91404
Specializes in epiphyllums and other tropical cacti.

North Jersey Bromeliads (12)
P.O. Box 181
Alpine, NJ 07620
Specializes in bromeliads.

Ben Haines (13)
1902 Lane
Topeka, KS 66604
Specializes in winter-hardy cacti and other succulents.

Hawk's Nursery (14)
2508 E. Vista Way
Vista, CA 92083
Specializes in epiphyllums.

Cactus by Mueller (15)
10411 Rosedale Highway
Bakersfield, CA 93308

Jessup's Cactus Nursery (16)
P.O. Box 327
Aromas, CA 95004

Apartment dwellers use a stair landing and space under the overhang for a small succulent collection.

Walther's Exotic House Plants (17)
R.D. 3, Box 30
Catskill, NY 12414
Specializes in bromeliads, cacti, and other succulents.

Loehman's Cactus Patch (18)
8014 Howe Street
P.O. Box 871
Paramount, CA 90723

Oakhill Gardens (19)
Route 3, Box 87
Dallas, OR 97338
Specializes in sedums and sempervivums.

Henrietta's Nursery (20)
1345 North Brawley
Fresno, CA 93711
Offers a large selection of cacti and succulents, including hybridized schlumbergeras.

Scotts Valley Cactus (21)
5311 Scotts Valley Drive
Scotts Valley, CA 95066

Fernwood Plants (22)
P.O. Box 268
Topanga, CA 90290

Cactus Gem Nursery (23)
10092 Mann Drive
Cupertino, CA 95014

K & L Cactus Nursery (24)
12712 Stockton Boulevard
Galt, CA 95632

Singer's Growing Things (25)
6385 Enfield Avenue
Reseda, CA 91335
Has a selection of unusual succulents, including stapeliads, mesembs, and cycads.

Linda Goodman's Sun Plants (26)
P.O. Box 20014
Riverside, CA 92516

Desert Plant Company (27)
P.O. Box 880
Marfa, TX 79843
Specializes in cacti.

Grote's Cactus Gardens (28)
13555 So. Leland Road
Oregon City, OR 97045

Sturtevant's Cactus and Succulent Nursery (29)
Arlington, OR 97812

Beahm's Epiphyllum Gardens (30)
2686 Paloma Street
Pasadena, CA 91107
Specializes in epiphyllums, rhipsalis, and hoyas.

Abbey Gardens (31)
176 Toro Canyon Road
Carpinteria, CA 93013
Has a large selection of succulents, including cacti and other specialty plants for collectors.

Lakeview Gardens (32)
Route 3, Box 447
Escondido, CA 92025
Specializes in bromeliads.

Whitestone Gardens, Ltd. (33)
The Cactus Houses
Sutton-under-Whitestonecliff
Thirsk, Yorkshire
England YO 72PZ

Ed Storms, Lithops (34)
4223 Pershing
Fort Worth, TX 76107

Offers an extensive selection of lithops and other mesembs; also some succulent specialty plants.

Ashwood Specialty Plants (35)
4629 Centinela Avenue
Los Angeles, CA 90066
Has a large selection, including tropical cacti and bromeliads.

Grigsby Cactus Gardens (36)
2326 & 2354 Bella Vista
Vista, CA 92083

"Cycadia" (37)
17337 Chase Street
Northridge, CA 91324
Specializes in rare African species.

Other special addresses

If you have difficulty locating pumice through a local merchant, try writing to the distributor:

American Pumice Products, Inc.
221 West Dyer Road
Santa Ana, CA 92707

Membership in the Cactus and Succulent Society and subscriptions to their journal are available from:

Cactus & Succulent Society Journal
Abbey Garden Press
P. O. Box 3010
Santa Barbara, CA 93105

Directory of Common Names

Use this listing to find the scientific name of a plant for which you know the common name.

A
African milk-barrel /*Euphorbia horrida*
African tree grape /*Cissus bainesii*
Agave cactus /*Leuchtenbergia principis*
Airplane plant /*Crassula falcata*

B
Baby jade /*Crassula argentea*
Baby-toes /*Fenestraria rhopalophylla*
Bald old-man /*Cephalocereus palmeri*
Barrel cactus /*Echinocactus grusonii*
Baseball Plant /*Euphorbia obesa*
Beaver-tail /*Opuntia basilaris*
Bishop's cap /*Astrophytum myriostigma*
Blue agave /*Agave tequilana*
Blue barrel cactus /*Ferocactus glaucescens*
Blue-candle, blue-flame /*Myrtillocactus geometrizans*
Boojum tree /*Fouquieria columnaris, Idria columnaris*
Boston beans /*Sedum stahii*
Botterboom /*Cotyledon paniculata*
Bunny-ears /*Opuntia microdasys*
Burn aloe /*Aloe barbadensis*
Button cactus /*Epithelantha micromeris*

C
Cactus geranium /*Pelargonium echinatum*
Calico-hearts /*Adromischus maculatus*
Cape aloe /*Aloe ferox*
Century plant /*Agave americana*
Chenille plant /*Echeveria pulvinata*
Christmas cactus /*Schlumbergera bridgesii*
Christmas-cheer /*Sedum × rubrotinctum*
Cinnamon cactus /*Opuntia microdasys 'Rufida'*
Cleftstone /*Pleiospilos nelii*
Climbing onion /*Bowiea volubilis*
Coach-whip /*Fouquieria splendens*
Cobweb houseleek /*Sempervivum arachnoideum*
Cocklebur /*Huernia pillansii*
Cocoon plant /*Senecio haworthii*
Common houseleek /*Sempervivum tectorum*
Coral cactus /*Mammillaria heyderi*
Corkscrew /*Euphorbia mammillaris* hybrids
Corncob /*Euphorbia submammillaris*
Cotton-ball /*Espostoa lanata*
Cow's horn /*Euphorbia grandicornis*
Crab cactus /*Schlumbergera truncata*
Crinkle-leaf-plant /*Adromischus cristatus*
Crown-of-thorns /*Euphorbia milii*
Curiosity plant /*Cereus peruvianus 'Monstrosus'*

D
Desert rose /*Adenium obesum*
Devil's-tongue /*Ferocactus latispinus*
Donkey's-tail /*Sedum morganianum*
Drunkard's dream /*Hatiora salicornioides*

E
Eagle-claws /*Echeveria horizonthalonius*
Elephant bush /*Portulacaria afra*
Elephant-foot tree /*Beaucarnea recurvata*
Elephant's foot /*Dioscorea elephantipes*
Elkhorn euphorbia /*Euphorbia lactea 'Cristata'*

F
Fairy-washboard /*Haworthia limifolia*
Feltbush /*Kalanchoe beharensis*
Flowering-stone /*Dinteranthus puberulus*
Fire-crown cactus /*Rebutia senilis*
Fishhook cactus /*Ferocactus wislizenii*

G
Giant-club /*Cereus peruvianus 'Monstrosus'*
Giant saguaro cactus /*Carnegiea gigantea*
Ghost plant /*Graptopetalum paraguayense*
Glory-of-Texas /*Thelocactus bicolor*
Golden barrel cactus /*Echinocactus grusonii*
Golden moss sedum /*Sedum acre*
Golden-tooth aloe /*Aloe nobilis*
Gooseberry kleina /*Senecio herreianus*
Green aloe /*Aloe barbadensis*

H
Hairy toad plant /*Stapelia hirsuta*
Hatchet cactus /*Pelecyphora asseliformis*
Hens-and-chicks /*Echeveria × imbricata*

J
Jade tree /*Crassula argentea*
Jewel plant /× *Pachyveria haagei*
Jewelled aloe /*Aloe distans*

K
Kangaroo rose /*Lapidaria margaretae*

L
Lace aloe /*Aloe aristata*
Large barrel cactus /*Echinocactus ingens, E. platycanthus*
Little-candles /*Mammillaria prolifera*
Living-baseball /*Euphorbia obesa*
Living-rock cactus /*Pleiospilos bolusii*

M
Medusa's-head /*Euphorbia caput-medusae*
Mexican giant barrel /*Echinocactus ingens*
Mimicry plant /*Pleiospilos bolusii*
Miniature wax plant /*Hoya bella*
Molded wax /*Echeveria agavoides*
Moss crassula /*Crassula lycopodioides*
Mother-of-pearl plant /*Graptopetalum paraguayense*

N
Night-blooming cereus /*Hylocereus undatus*

O
Ocotillo /*Fouquieria splendens*
Old-man cactus /*Cephalocereus senilis*
Old-man-of-the-Andes /*Borzicactus trollii, Oreocereus trollii*
Old-man-of-the-mountains /*Borzicactus celsianus*
Orchid cacti /*Epiphyllum* spp.
Organ-pipe cactus /*Lemaireocereus marginatus, L. thurberi*
Owl-eyes /*Mammillaria parkinsonii*

P
Painted-lady /*Echeveria derenbergii*
Panda plant /*Kalanchoe tomentosa*
Peanut cactus /*Chamaecereus sylvestri*
Pearl echeveria /*Echeveria elegans*
Pencil-leaf /*Gasteria caespitosa*
Peruvian apple /*Cereus peruvianus*
Peruvian old-man /*Espostoa lanata*
Pinwheel plant /*Aeonium haworthii*
Plover-eggs /*Adromischus cooperii*
Plush plant /*Echeveria pulvinanta*
Polka-dot cactus /*Opuntia microdasys 'Albispina'*
Ponytail /*Beaucarnea recurvata*
Powder-blue cereus /*Lamaireocereus pruinosis*

Echeveria hybrid

Princess-of-the-night / *Selenicereus pteranthus*
Prism cactus / *Leuchtenbergia principis*
Pussy-ears / *Kalanchoe tomentosa*

Q

Queen-of-the-night / *Hylocereus undatus, Selenicereus grandiflorus*
'Queen of the Night' orchid cactus / *Epiphyllum oxypetalum*

R

Rabbit-ears / *Opuntia microdasys*
Rattail cactus / *Aporocactus flagelliformis*
Rattail crassula / *Crassula lycopodioides*
Rattlesnake / *Crassula teres*
Red bunny-ears / *Opuntia microdasys* 'Rufida'
Red-crown / *Rebutia minuscula*
Red dragon flower / *Heurnia schneiderana*
Redondo creeper / *Lampranthus filicaulis*
Rosary vine / *Ceropegia woodii*
Rose-pincushion / *Mammillaria zeilmanniana*

S

Sago palm / *Cycas revoluta*
Scarlet barrel cactus / *Notocactus haselbergii*
Scarlet bugler / *Cleistocactus baumannii*
Scarlet crown cactus / *Rebutia grandiflora*
Scarlet-paint-brush / *Crassula falcata*
Sea-urchin cactus / *Astrophytum asterias*
Seven-stars / *Ariocarpus retusus*
Silver-crown / *Cotyledon undulata*
Silver cluster cactus / *Mammillaria prolifera*
Silver jade plant / *Crassula aborescens*
Silver torch / *Cleistocactus strausii*
Snowball cactus / *Mammillaria bocasana* 'Inermis'
South American old man / *Borzicactus celsianus*

Spanish moss / *Tillandsia usneoides*
Spice cactus / *Hatiora salicornioides*
Spider aloe / *Aloe humilis*
Spider cactus / *Gymnocalycium denudatum*
Splitrock / *Pleiospilos nelii*
Star cactus / *Astrophytum cornatum*
Strawberry cactus / *Echinocereus enneacanthus* 'Conglomeratus'
String-of-beads / *Senecio rowleyanus*
String-of-buttons / *Crassula perforata*
Sweetheart geranium / *Pelargonium echinatum*

T

Thanksgiving cactus / *Schlumbergera truncata*
Thick plant / *Pachyphytum compactum*
Tiger aloe / *Aloe variegata*
Tiger's-jaws / *Faucaria tigrina*
Tiny living rocks / *Lithops* species
Tom-thumb / *Parodia aureispina*
Torch cactus / *Trichocereus spachianus*
Torch plant / *Aloe aristata*
Trailing ice plant / *Lampranthus spectabilis*
Turk's cap cactus / *Melocactus intortus*

V

Veldt grape / *Cissus quadrangula, C. quadrangularis*
Velvetleaf / *Kalanchoe beharensis*
Violet sea-urchin / *Acanthocalycium violaceum*

W

Wax plant / *Hoya carnosa*
Window plant / *Fenestraria rhopalophylla*

Z

Zebra haworthia / *Haworthia fasciata*
Zygocactus / *Schlumbergera bridgesii*

Index

Boldface numbers refer to main entries. Numbers in italics refer to illustrations. Common names are listed on pages 140–141 with corresponding botanical names for easy reference in the index.